[RE]CREATE

THE

Leadership
and Design for
Sustainable
Excellence

ORGANIZATION
YOU REALLY
WANT!

JOHN R. LATHAM, PH.D.

Permissions Department
Organization Design Studio, Ltd.
P.O. Box 64319
Colorado Springs, Colorado
80962
U.S.A.

To order books visit: http://www.OrganizationDesignStudio.com

Printed in the United States of America.

ISBN: 978-0-9981491-1-0 (Paperback)

For Penny

CONTENTS

LIST OF FIGURES

ACKNOWLEDGEMENTS

Without the support of my wife Penny, this book would not exist. So my first debt of gratitude is to her and my family and friends for their support. In particular, I want to thank Dr. Chad McAllister for his friendship and constant encouragement to get this project done!

This book was inspired by numerous leaders, colleagues, consultants, and scholars who over the years generously took the time to help me better understand the complex nature of leadership and organization design.

Without the participation of the award-winning leaders, the research that led to the development of the leadership framework would not have been possible. This book combines that research with many other ideas and concepts from practice that I learned from many leaders and colleagues over the years including other performance excellence award examiners and consultants.

In addition, this work builds on the research and writings of many scholars - only some of which are cited in the book. I am sure there are many more that I didn't think to include – I apologize.

I also want to thank Dr. Ron Schulingkamp for his tireless reviews of early drafts and valuable feedback.

Thank you!

FOREWORD

I have had the good fortune to spend the last 25+ years of my professional life working with and learning from many outstanding organizations, leaders, researchers, and mentors. As a practitioner and a researcher, my work is focused on learning how high-performing organizations work and how leaders successfully [re]design and transform them to achieve sustainable excellence. Two award-winning, peer-reviewed frameworks have emerged – one for leadership and one for design. These two frameworks provide leaders of organizations with a structured approach for creating and sustaining high-performance.

The leadership framework emerged from practice and research with CEOs who successfully led transformations that resulted in recognition as recipients of the Malcolm Baldrige National Quality Award (Latham, 2013a; 2013b). I chose the Baldrige recipients because they produce ever-improving value for multiple stakeholders including customers, employees, investors, suppliers and partners, society, and the natural environment. The CEO quotes in this book are from in-depth interviews with these successful leaders of sustainable excellence.

Reaching your organization's full potential requires organization and managerial systems that are custom tailored to your unique situation. The design framework guides you through the process using a flexible approach to [re]design any organization system, process, or practice (Latham, 2012). When combined, these frameworks form a **blueprint** to guide your journey to sustainable excellence.

I hope this blueprint helps you *[Re]Create the Organization You Really Want!*

Enjoy the journey!

John Latham, Ph.D.

INTRODUCTION

Leading the Transformation to Sustainable Excellence

THE CHALLENGE

Leaders today face increasing demands from a variety of stakeholders. The challenge is to figure out a way to create value for all the key stakeholders without taking from one to serve another.

Pressures from stakeholders combined with increasing competition and advances in technology provide many dilemmas but many opportunities for the organization designer. We must get beyond the attitude of a zero-sum game and self-serving silos and create organizations with systems and cultures of service.

In other words, we need leaders who can design organizations that create value for multiple stakeholders.

Raising the Bar

The bar is continually being raised, and the definition of success for all types of organizations (profit-seeking, non-profit, government, etc.) is continuously changing and increasingly complex. Truth be told, organization performance has never been all that good — at least not compared to its potential. It seems that about the time we figure out a good way to run the organization, the world changes on us.

It is a bit of a cliché to say we live in times of great change, but the speed and scale of change do seem to be increasing. Our organizational models and theories are not keeping pace, and the successful modern organization architect is living on the leading edge of knowledge and creativity. We now have new technologies that enable a variety of designs for the organization of the 21ˢᵗ century. It is an exciting time to be an organization designer.

Brief History

A leader's work is never done: organization design is a never-ending process of creation, refinement, and recreation. From the mid-1940s to the 1970s, the pent-up demand and limited global competition allowed many business leaders to focus mainly on financial results. The party ended sometime around 1980 when Xerox woke up to a situation where the Japanese were selling copiers in the U.S. for what it cost Xerox to make them (Kotter and Heskett, 1992). During the 1980s, product quality became a key success factor and was directly linked to market and financial success.

In the beginning, many proposed that high quality was simply too expensive. However, we eventually discovered that high quality resulted in reduced cost and increased market share — or as Phillip Crosby wrote in a book of the same title: *Quality is Free.*

As the service and knowledge worker industries increased in size and importance, they discovered that talented, passionate people are also a key to high quality, customer satisfaction, and financial performance. During the 1990s, successful organizations became quite good at connecting these dots or as Federal Express called it — "people, service, profit" (AMA 1991). The bar has been raised once again to include sustainable results in three key areas — financial, environmental, and societal — or as Elkington, Emerson, and Beloe (2006) call it, the "triple bottom line."

Similar sequences play out in other parts of the world where industries and sometimes entire economies are disrupted.

Today there is a growing backlash against globalization including a recent vote for the United Kingdom (UK) to leave the European Union (EU). The underlying issues related to increasing pressure from multiple stakeholders are common and widespread. These issues are compounded by increased competition and advances in digital technology.

Stakeholder Pressure

Leaders are feeling increasing pressure from a variety of stakeholders (workforce, customers, investors, etc.), all of whom seem to have an opinion on how leaders should run their organizations. You may sometimes feel like everyone wants a piece of you. Many leaders express frustration with the seemingly insatiable needs and desires of their stakeholders. Some days it seems like nothing is ever enough. Many leaders find themselves with more and more to do, but with less time and resources to do it. This more-for-less situation is a consistent theme across the multiple groups that have a stake in the organization. The future belongs to organizations that can figure out how to create ever-improving value for all six groups: the workforce, customers, investors, suppliers and partners, the community, and the natural environment. In other words, successful leaders are making money in a way that is consistent with a sustainable society and a sustainable planet.

Six Stakeholder Groups

Each of the six stakeholder groups has their own perspective and needs. According to Gallup, the majority of the workforce is looking for other opportunities and few are engaged in their current work. The dissatisfied **workforce** is serving

customers who always want more for less, and competitors help raise the bar. To make matters worse, **investors** are nervous, and many are cautiously holding back reserves vs. investing in the improvements needed to succeed in the next decade and beyond. This pressure isn't limited to for-profit investors. Non-profit donors are asking for more and more impact for their donor dollar, and taxpayers are asking for more and more services for less tax burden.

There is an old saying regarding **suppliers and partners**: "Garbage in, garbage out." Squeezing suppliers on price results in fewer resources for supplier improvement: a downward spiral that is counterproductive to both parties. Society also puts pressure on us to perform in ways that do not detract from the **community**. They find their voice through an increasing menu of media and government policies.

Finally, the **natural environment** and future generations find a voice in the other five stakeholder groups. While still a minority, many customers are choosing products that are environmentally friendly and produced by companies that are socially responsible. This tendency is likely to increase over time. Also, investors have recognized the risks associated with environmental and social issues. Many employees are choosing where they spend their career based on the social responsibility values and record.

Unfortunately, most of our organizations are not designed to create value for all these stakeholders.

Increasing Competition

Organizations today are feeling pressure to change from one or more of the six stakeholder groups. This is both a crisis and an opportunity. The crisis is there is an endless supply of competitors willing to address the needs of the stakeholders and take market share. Unfortunately, many "organizations are like VCRs blinking 12:00. They are poorly designed, out of date and ill-prepared to survive, let alone thrive, in the modern environment" (Latham, 2013c). However, if the competitors can do it, so can you. That is the challenge AND the opportunity.

You can [re]create your organization or parts of your organization to produce better products and services for less money, manpower, and impact on the environment. This dissatisfaction is a useful impetus to help overcome the inertia of the status quo. The crisis is the "burning platform" described in the leading change literature. You know you need to jump, but which direction do you go?

While dissatisfaction is an important forcing function, overcoming inertia requires the combined tension of dissatisfaction and a compelling directive or vision of the desired reality. In other words, the combined pressure from dissatisfaction with the status quo and the compelling vision must be greater than the resistance to change or inertia. The good news is this pressure is useful. These stakeholder pressures and other sources of dissatisfaction are pushing you to change and change for the better.

Technology Changes

At the same time that leaders face increasing pressure to create value for multiple stakeholders, we also are experiencing a shift in how we do business. Advances in digital technology are enabling new business models, systems, and processes. We now find ourselves in the middle of a major digital transformation of organizations.

"Organizations today face increasing pressure from multiple stakeholders and relentless global competition, forcing them to become more innovative in everything they do and produce" (Latham, 2013c).

Like the other pressures, this transformation offers both crisis and opportunity. The crisis is we might be left behind and lose market share if our competitors beat us to the new models and systems. The opportunity is we now have organization design options that were not possible even a few years ago.

Form follows function, and many of our organizations and their systems are designed for another century. All too often we add technology on top of existing processes, creating a surface layer of digital capability on a poor design. To fully address the challenges we face, we need to rethink the design of our organizations, systems, and processes to ensure they are aligned with an effective strategy. That is going to require a new attitude.

New Attitude

When you add up all these demands, it can feel a bit overwhelming. You might be thinking, "No matter what I do, it is never enough!" It is frustrating and can feel like you are failing. To move forward, we need to consciously shift our self-image from victim to servant.

The first step is to recognize that you have the same ultimate goals as the stakeholders in that they need you to be successful. This is what Dr. Joe Alexander did at Monfort College of Business, a 2004 Malcolm Baldrige Award Recipient at the University of Northern Colorado. Dr. Alexander's team was feeling pressures from a wide variety of stakeholders, including students, parents, business owners (eventual employers), accrediting bodies, and even state and federal regulatory agencies. So the college transformed adversarial relationships into partnerships working toward the same goals and objectives.

According to Dr. Alexander, the key benefit in changing those stakeholder relationships was freeing the stakeholders up from having to "police" the college into meeting a minimum standard, since the standard that college had already set for itself far exceeded anything the stakeholders would have ever expected of them. That was the key in building a more collegial partnership. Many organizations find themselves at odds with their stakeholders, especially regulatory agencies. The challenge is to reframe and transform these combative relationships into partnerships. A similar internal issue often holds organizations back.

Self-Serving Silos

A new attitude is essential but not sufficient when transforming an organization. Even with the new attitude, many of our organizations are still chaotic, complex, confusing, and characterized by a collection of "self-serving silos." One problem with this ad hoc situation is it is not consistent and repeatable, and thus there is low performance, little learning, and limited improvement. If the internal culture consists of islands of activity, each out for themselves, it is difficult to develop a partnership with external stakeholders. The self-serving silos have to be integrated into a team of coordinated efforts, all focused on serving the customer or someone in the organization who is serving the customer.

Given that many change efforts fail to achieve the desired results, you may be doubting that it is really possible to fix the silos that sub-optimize (in other words, harm) the organization for their benefit. A few CEOs in our study doubted that they could pull it off, but they never doubted that it was the right thing to do and eventually they succeeded.

Approaches to Improvement

You may be thinking, "This is just another improvement initiative in the long line of initiatives, so what makes this one different?" Most organizations have tried many different approaches (fads) to improve performance. There are many approaches to improvement to choose from including Six Sigma, Lean, Lean-Six Sigma, Appreciative Inquiry, and more recently Design Thinking, so on and so forth.

While the results from these approaches are mixed, they all work, sometimes. One issue that limits the success of these approaches is they are often applied piecemeal in an attempt to improve the bits and pieces of the organization without sufficient consideration of the larger context, systems, and strategy. Another issue is the changes are often incremental when more substantial changes are needed to get the desired results. The design approach to organization improvement presented here integrates key aspects of previous approaches and adds additional considerations that enable a leap in performance. In addition, the organization design approach to improvement facilitates a new design that creates value for multiple stakeholders —
or win-win.

Win-win

The creation of value for ALL key stakeholders is a requirement for sustainable excellence and a core leadership responsibility. In other words, designing an organization that creates "win-win" for all stakeholders vs. taking from one to serve another.

The good news is a zero-sum game of trade-offs is not needed to create value for multiple stakeholders. High-performing organizations take a systems approach to design that focuses on developing a workforce that creates and delivers great products and services that result in satisfied customers who buy more and tell their friends, improving the top line and making the investors happy. Also, systems thinking enables organization designs that create value for other key stakeholders such as suppliers and partners, society, and the environment.

This requires a design philosophy where "Yes is more." Bjarke Ingels is a "starchitect" who has built a successful career working to include multiple stakeholders into his building designs. His philosophy of "Yes is more" is a practical approach to creating what you might call "utopian architecture." The challenge for organization architects is to figure out ways to design the organization so as to say "yes" to the needs, wants, and desires of the multiple stakeholders. If we can design and build buildings that meet the needs of multiple stakeholders, we should be able to do the same with organizations. And many organizations with the help of performance excellence criteria have done just that.

So the challenge is to [re]create our organizations so that they create ever-improving value for multiple stakeholders including the workforce, customers, investors, suppliers and partners, society, and the natural environment. If we are to meet the organization design challenge, we first need to understand the key components of organization design.

ORGANIZATION DESIGN

When many people hear the words "design" and "designer" they often think of fashion, interior design, or the design of everyday items such as glasses, salt shakers, and so forth. However, everything that is not created by nature is designed by humans (consciously or unconsciously). Thus, our human-created organizations can be purposefully designed or redesigned to produce even greater value for the multiple stakeholders.

Unlike buildings or objects, organizations are concepts and sometimes difficult to make fully explicit. Organization designs consist of artifacts that convey information about the context, culture, and systems. Artifacts take many forms from diagrams and descriptions of systems to visual displays of data to organizational symbols. To help understand the design of organizations we focus on the tangible artifacts (Figure I-1). In this case the artifacts include the tangible objects and communication media from four cornerstones (stakeholders, strategy, systems, and scorecard), the culture (rituals, heroes, and symbols), and the context of the organization, including physical environment and the external operating environment. These artifacts, including the less tangible words and deeds of leaders, are what members of the organization see and hear, think and feel, and ultimately say and do (behavior).

Figure I-1 Organization Design Components

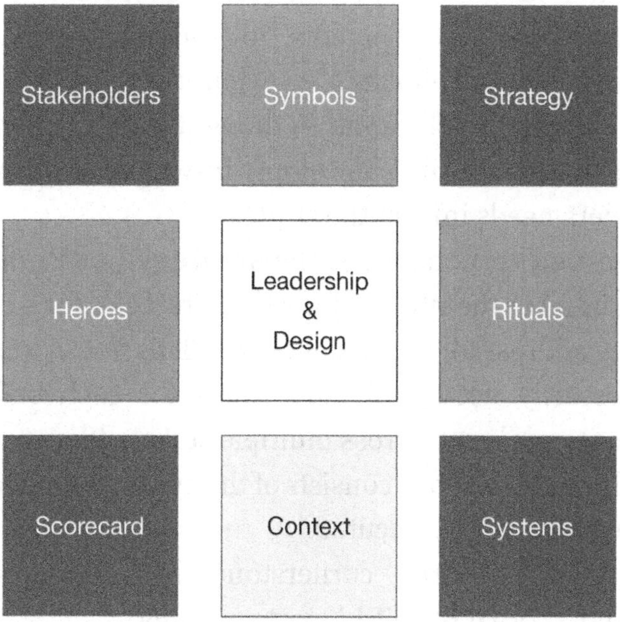

Stakeholders	Symbols	Strategy
Heroes	Leadership & Design	Rituals
Scorecard	Context	Systems

Cornerstones

The four cornerstones of organization design are stakeholders, strategy, systems, and scorecard. While the four components are all interrelated, there is a logical sequence to help you think about the alignment of these components. Stakeholder needs and desires inform the development of strategies for both products and the organization design. Strategies produce both external products and services as well as organization system changes to effectively produce and deliver those products and services. Finally, a comprehensive scorecard measures how well the systems and products are working, how the strategy is progressing, along with the value created for the multiple stakeholders. All four cornerstones are manifested in artifacts including documents, speeches, etc.

The first cornerstone is **stakeholders** — or the WHO of organization design and the basis for organization alignment. There are three key elements to this cornerstone. First, understand the stakeholders — what they need and want. Second, empathize with them — thoughtfully consider what it is like to be them. Third, develop win-win relationships. The stakeholders needs inform the strategy.

The second cornerstone is the **strategy** (goals, objectives, and priorities) or the WHAT. Effective strategies for sustainable excellence address all the stakeholders. This doesn't mean that you necessarily need individual goals for each stakeholder group. Some goals cut-across multiple stakeholders.

The third cornerstone consists of the **systems** and processes — or HOW strategy is executed.

Finally, the fourth cornerstone is a comprehensive **scorecard** — or HOW WELL you are doing.

"Comprehensive" means the scorecard measures the system performance, strategy progress, and the stakeholder value and satisfaction. These four cornerstones provide a solid foundation for the journey to sustainable excellence.

However, this foundation is only as strong as the alignment and linkages between the cornerstones. The cornerstones need to be consistent and congruent. The focus on stakeholder needs and relationships helps provide a common alignment point for strategy, execution, and learning and innovation. Also, a systems perspective combined with design thinking provides the basis for organization designs that create value for multiple stakeholders.

These four cornerstones are inert without people to make them come alive. The culture fills in the spaces between the cornerstones and help to bring the inert cornerstones to life.

Culture

The four cornerstones are held together by a culture of excellence and innovation. The culture brings these four key components to life and provides the energy to move the organization forward. To achieve and sustain excellence the key culture elements — including values, rituals, heroes, and symbols — have to be aligned with the stakeholders, strategy, systems, and scorecard.

When I ask successful leaders of organization transformation what they would do differently next time, the most common response is they would have aligned the organization sooner because that was where the real power was. The challenge we face with culture is the values of an organization are not directly visible. Our values can't be observed directly. We infer values through their manifestations — behaviors, decisions, priorities, etc. Values are inferred from how people act (practices) and the rituals, heroes, and symbols of the organization that are visible and audible.

As Mom used to say, "Choose your friends wisely." The corollary for organizations might be, "Choose your heroes wisely."

Your heroes' behavior (what they say and do) is a powerful message. Heroes are those individuals the organization holds up as the epitome of success in the organization. These are the people they tell stories about. They are legends. The second tangible element of culture are the symbols. There are symbols throughout our organization that tell us what is important and valued (e.g., reserved parking spots). In addition, organizations have a wide variety of rituals from executive retreats to Friday afternoon beer busts. Rituals are designed to create thoughts and feelings in the participants' minds that influence the desired behavior.

The task is to select heroes and design symbols and rituals that send messages that are aligned with our desired organization and values. Some have tried to separate culture from the other components of organization design such as strategy. However, all the components work together as an integrated whole and the design and results are context dependent.

Context

Context is a key consideration when designing any aspect of the organization. For example, the most appropriate strategy development and deployment system might be very different for a Fortune 100 with operations in 40 countries vs. a mom-and-pop coffee shop with two locations in one city. Context contains important information including the facilities, the technology, the type of work (e.g., nuclear power vs. education), the workforce, and the purpose and mission of the organization. The cornerstone and culture components need to align with and fit the unique characteristics of your organization. These all have to make sense together with the type of work you do, your facilities, the geography, etc.

Alignment

The bad news is many of our organizations are hodge-podges of ill-fitting pieces, making it difficult to create value for any stakeholders. The good news is organizations were designed by humans and thus can be redesigned.

While low-performing organizations are chaotic, complex, and confusing, high- performing organization are aligned and congruent. Four key elements must be aligned and integrated for any major change effort to succeed: stakeholder needs, strategy (goals and objectives), the action plans along with resources, and the performance measures (scorecard). In fact, the alignment and integration of the cornerstones with the organizational culture may be the most important facilitator of organization [re]design and transformation. Alignment and integration determine the degree to which the four cornerstones are consistent and working together with the culture in the same direction.

For our purposes, *organization design is a stakeholder-centered approach to aligning and integrating the systems, strategy, and scorecard with the organization's culture and the unique context.*

Why Organization Design?

So why do we focus on organization design? There is an old saying, "You can't get flowers to grow by pulling on them." The components of organization design are what people see and hear. What they see and hear influences what they think and how they feel. What they think and feel influences what they say and do or their behavior. Their behavior influences organization performance (Figure I-2).

Figure I-2 Why Organization Design?

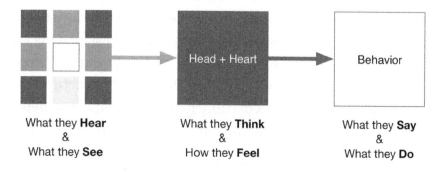

What they **Hear**	What they **Think**	What they **Say**
&	&	&
What they **See**	How they **Feel**	What they **Do**

We focus on organization design because it influences the behavior of those who work in and with the organization. Stakeholders experience the organization's many processes and practices, interactions, and artifacts. While interacting with the organization, stakeholders hear and see many manifestations of the organization design. William McDonough proposes that "Design is the first signal of human intention." But whose intent?

Organization Architect

Like architects of buildings, organization architects must leverage what we know (the science) of organizations and systems with what is possible and not yet imagined (the art) to develop solutions that address many constraints and the needs of multiple stakeholders.

There are two main types of organization architects (OAs) — formal leaders and the informal leaders who help them. Formal leaders include those leading existing organizations that need to be redesigned and entrepreneurs who are designing the organization for this first time. These are the individuals with the power and responsibility to change how the organization operates. In addition, there are a variety of OAs who are informal leaders such as internal subject matter experts (SMEs) and external consultants who help the formal leaders.

Both formal and informal leader OAs must be able to lead across functional boundaries in order to be successful. OAs are found at all levels of the organization, and their design efforts range from processes to systems to the overall structure and business model. What is needed to achieve sustainable excellence is for leaders to become architects of their organizations and

[re]imagine and [re]invent them to create value for multiple stakeholders.

As Gary Hamel noted in his book *The Future of Management,* "What is lacking is not insightful analysis, but truly bold and imaginative alternatives to the management status quo— and an army of innovators who have the stamina to reinvent management from the ground up."

> *"Successful leaders in the future will have to become architects of enduring organizations by designing systems that create sustainable results for multiple stakeholders"* (Latham, 2012).

Mind of the Organization Architect

The mind of the OA is multi-dimensional and includes perspectives from multiple disciplines. The OA integrates practical, creative, and human dimensions to develop holistic designs that create value for multiple stakeholders. The OA is practical and incorporates engineering and business mindsets. At the same time, the OA uses research to inform the technical design of systems to produce the value intended. Also, the systems must make financial sense. In other words, they must produce value — more value in output than the input. The OA also incorporates human dimensions both individuals and groups.

As part psychologist, the OA incorporates insights from psychology into the design of systems. The OA is also part anthropologist incorporating how individuals work together and develop cultural norms. Finally, the complete OA is a creative designer that incorporates the possibilities of art and design into developing new and imaginative designs. This multi-disciplinary perspective informs the two basic OA competencies of leadership and design. Regardless of position or title, organization architects (leaders, entrepreneurs, and those who help them) must master two skills — leading transformation and organization design.

Leadership

The journey to sustainable excellence is challenging and uncertain. Most change efforts fail to achieve their objectives mainly because leaders fail to set the example and personally see it through. The first step in the journey is for leaders to begin with themselves. As Gandhi proposed, you must become the change you want to see in the organization. Only then will you be credible.

Setting the example requires you understand and apply the five key components of the leading transformation framework: forces and facilitators of change, leadership system, leadership style, culture, and the individual leader. The Leadership Framework presented here is based on the experiences of CEOs who led successful organization transformations that created sustainable value for multiple stakeholders (Latham, 2013a, 2013b). The flexible framework includes a design framework to help OAs [re]design the organization one design project at a time.

Design

Leaders today face many challenges that require the design or redesign of organizational structures, systems, and processes to achieve and sustain high performance. Reaching your organization's full potential demands organization and managerial systems that are custom-tailored to your unique situation. Best practices from other companies, consultants, and business books often work, yet they seldom achieve the high levels of performance possible with a "bespoke" (custom) solution.

The Design Framework guides you through the five phases of discovery, design, develop, deploy, and iterate (D4 + I) using a flexible approach for designing or redesigning any organization system, process, or practice (Latham, 2012). While the framework components are presented in sequence, the actual use of the framework is often an iterative give and take between the individual components. The first eight discovery components provide a springboard to the creative design process.

Organization system redesign is a common strategy deployment activity. Unfortunately, many organizations are much better at strategy development than they are at strategy deployment. The Design Framework increases the odds of successful and sustainable strategy deployment. The remainder of the book is organized around these two frameworks.

LEADERSHIP & DESIGN BLUEPRINT

Leading the journey to sustainable excellence requires the flexible combination of leveraging the forces and facilitators of change with leadership activities and behaviors, organizational culture, and individual leader characteristics. The Leadership & Design Blueprint integrates the Design Framework into the Leadership Framework providing a 14-step guide to [re] design and transform your organizations to achieve sustainable excellence.

The Leadership Framework is composed of five major components divided into 14 components (Figure I-3). Our exploration of the framework begins with the forces for change (1) and ends with the facilitators for change or journey (14). Leaders who have successfully led organizations to achieve sustainable excellence focused their time on nine key activities (Latham, 2013a, 2013b). These nine key activities form a leadership system (2-10). Leadership is part art and part science; the leadership system is the science of leading transformation.

Figure I-3 Leadership and Design Blueprint

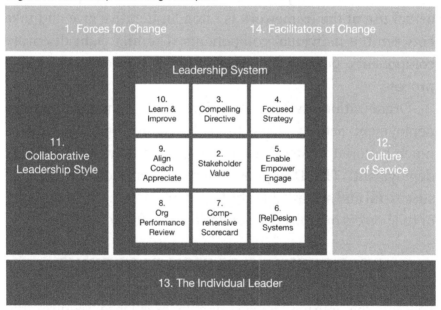

The leadership system is the centerpiece of the Leadership Framework, and stakeholder value is the centerpiece (focus) of the leadership system. The leadership system is composed of nine interrelated components that describe WHAT leaders do. While these are presented in sequence, the actual use of the leadership system is often iterative, and you can begin and end anywhere on a given day.

The center of the system is an understanding of stakeholders and their needs, wants, and desires. This understanding informs all eight other components starting with the compelling directive that incorporates the stakeholders (2) into the purpose, mission, vision, and values of the organization (3). This directive, in turn, is the starting point for the development of a focused strategy (4) that will address the stakeholder requirements.

Once the foundation is established, the workforce is enabled, empowered, and engaged (5) to carry out the strategy in a way that is consistent with the compelling directive. Also, this workforce executes the operations of the organization to deliver the products and services in a way that creates value for the multiple stakeholders. At the same time, they continuously improve the organization systems and processes by designing and redesigning them to improve performance (6). The success of the strategies, people, and systems is measured by a comprehensive scorecard (7) that provides feedback on both the performance and the progress in each area.

This information is then analyzed and reviewed as part of a collaborative performance review process (8) that translates the information into a deeper understanding of the organization and informs changes to operations and strategy. Based on the organization performance review, individual performance is reinforced with rewards and recognition as well as remediation (9). The last component is a continuous learning and improvement process (10) that is embedded into all the key systems and processes.

The leadership system is energized by the collaborative leadership style (11) that describes HOW leaders do the activities in the leadership system. These activities and behaviors become embedded into the culture of service (12) that increases the sustainability of the transformation. The individual leader (13) often has to personally change to be credible and effective. Finally, the journey (14) is planned, tracked, managed, and adjusted to achieve sustainable excellence.

The journey is never over, which some might find discouraging — but denying it doesn't change the facts.

1. Forces for Change

While the motivation for change varies widely, there must be enough tension to overcome the inertia of satisfaction with the status quo. The framework starts with identifying the forces of change specific to your organization and context. What are the external "pushing" forces for change? What are the "pulling" forces of change? What is the vision of a new desired future? Are these sufficient to overcome the inertia of the status quo? How can you leverage these forces to move your organization forward?

2. Stakeholder Value

The focus of a transformation to sustainable excellence is to increase the value created for multiple stakeholders including the workforce, customers, investors, suppliers and partners, community, and environment. The focus on stakeholder needs and relationships helps provide a common alignment point for the strategy, systems, scorecard, and overall organization design for sustainable excellence. In short, high-performing organizations create an efficient system and value for other stakeholders such as suppliers and partners, society, and the environment. The task here is to understand the stakeholders' needs and desires.

3. Compelling Directive

The needs of the stakeholders inform the creation of a "compelling directive." The format of the compelling directive varies but typically consists of the organization's purpose, mission, vision, and values. The vision describes the desired reality. The vision is an essential part of creating positive tension, a key force of change to overcome resistance to change. The compelling directive builds a bridge between the stakeholders and the strategy.

4. Focused Strategy

How will the organization achieve the desired reality described in the compelling directive? The focused strategy translates the compelling directive and stakeholders' needs into more specific goals, objectives, and clear expectations. The key here is to focus on a FEW key goals at a particular point in time. Some organization transformations require hundreds of changes. Success depends on picking just a few of those to work on at a time and then actually executing the plan, then working on the next priorities as the journey unfolds. The focused strategy is continuously evolving to meet the current requirements and challenges. The focused strategy aligns the priorities through the organization and provides the foundation to enable, empower, and engage the workforce.

5. Enable, Empower, Engage

While many leaders claim that their people are their most important asset, their actions often tell a different story. High-performing organizations develop and engage their workforce to accomplish the strategy. Creating an engaged workforce consists of (a) acquiring and placing talent, (b) developing (enabling) and empowering people, (c) involving and engaging the workforce at all levels, and (d) addressing the whole person. Acquiring and retaining the best talent is a challenge for most organizations. The best people will only work for organizations where they feel valued, enjoy their work, and achieve their full potential in a win-win arrangement. Note: If you don't need the best people, then consider automating the work.

6. [Re]Design Systems

The focused strategy also drives the implementation of action plans to accomplish the strategy. There are typically two types of strategy deployment projects — those focused on new products and services and those focused on building the organization systems to develop, produce, deliver, and the products and services. Even new product launches are organization systems that need to be designed or redesigned to achieve the particular goal. The deployment of the strategy focuses on the [re]design and further development of one or more key systems to achieve an objective. The Design Framework combined with a focus on system design provides the structure to design, develop, and deploy any new or redesigned initiative or system in the organization. The only way we know if our redesign efforts are actually improving performance is to measure performance.

7. Comprehensive Scorecard

The progress and performance improvements resulting from the deployment of the action plans are measured and tracked by a comprehensive scorecard that measures the stakeholders, strategy, and systems. The comprehensive scorecard goes beyond a simple bottom line to a deeper understanding of the organization as a system. This includes both current performance and the performance trends over time. Measuring performance and comparing your organization's performance to other high-performing organizations helps create dissatisfaction with the status quo and is a key part of creating tension: productive tension. The scorecard is designed to facilitate a dialogue during the periodic organization performance reviews.

8. Organization Performance Review

Scorecard results are analyzed and periodically reviewed by the leaders at all levels who then revise the action plans and operations as necessary to accomplish the strategy. While much of the learning during these reviews is limited to single-loop learning and keeping things on track, occasionally the dialogue will result in an examination of the underlying assumptions and double-loop learning that enables the team to address root causes and prevent similar future problems. This fact-based approach to management includes organization performance analysis that informs the reinforcement of the desired behaviors.

9. Align, Coach, Appreciate

There is an old saying, "What gets measured gets done and what gets rewarded gets repeated." Reinforcing behavior is based on progress towards the overall strategy and includes recognition, rewards, promotions, and sometimes the removal of individuals. All too often, incentive systems are counter-productive and drive behaviors that are inconsistent with the overall compelling directive and strategy. So caution is warranted when evaluating and incentivizing performance. High-performing organizations align their incentives to ensure individual performance is supporting the best overall system performance.

10. Learn and Improve

Successful leaders of transformation are never satisfied with the organization's performance and learn from experience. To fully develop the organization's systems, culture, and individuals requires that the organization learn not only from their successes but also from their failures. Organizations that have achieved sustainable excellence by learning from success and failure did so using four common methods or approaches: strategic management cycle, organization assessment and improvement, continuous improvement, and benchmarking. These methods are often integrated into the other eight leadership system components.

    This description presents the nine activities in a sequence (2 through 10). However, leading an organization transformation is not a linear process. Think about the leadership system of nine activities as a flexible framework that can be entered and exited at any place in the system. How a leader implements these nine activities varies and depends on the design of each system component and the leadership style. In the coming chapters, we will focus on each of the nine leadership system components.

11. Collaborative Leadership Style

The framework offers leader behaviors that support the leadership system to achieve sustainable excellence. You might consider these the art of leading transformation — or HOW leaders accomplished the activities.

The collaborative style includes nine behaviors. Leaders establish their credibility by role modeling the behaviors and actions they want to see in the new organization. Organization architect leaders respect everyone, which helps them develop collaborative relationships to [re]design and transform the organization. OAs are great communicators and deliver a consistent message regardless of the situation. At the same time, they hold people accountable for the changes. They are systems thinkers who are always learning from their personal involvement in the design and change activities. It is a style that helps people create the organization that they want. This style along with the activities shapes the culture.

12. Culture of Service

Ultimately, sustaining excellence requires that the new systems, processes, and practices become habitual and embedded in the culture. Culture is composed of values and norms that are manifested in the rituals, heroes, and symbols. Organizations that have achieved sustainable excellence have five cultural characteristics in common. They are a complementary combination of valued employees who trust each other and work as a team. At the same time, this trusting team is focused on delivering excellence to the customer. In the end, individuals working together are the essence of any sustainable change.

13. The Individual Leader

Organization architects have five common characteristics that increase the odds of achieving and sustaining high performance:

purpose and meaning, humility tempered by confidence, integrity, systems perspective, and motivational and attitudinal patterns. While the other leadership components of system and style are visible and observable, this one is below the surface. What would it take to make this leadership style authentic for you? What motivates you to do the key activities?

14. Facilitators of Change

Some leaders of successful change doubted they could do it. It can seem overwhelming. There are a few key facilitators of change to help you along the journey. First, you are not alone so start by developing your team of organization architects. Second, begin with the senior leadership team so you will have credibility and the personal knowledge to lead the journey. Then develop a plan to guide your [re]design and transformation. There is an old saying, "If it has been done, it must be possible."

There are lots of great examples recognized as role-model organizations by the Malcolm Baldrige Award and other awards around the world. As Nelson Mandela put it, "It always seems impossible until it's done."

THE PRIZE

What do we expect to get out of all this? First, the leadership and design approach is a more direct route to the goal of sustainable excellence than other options. Second, the direct route results in a faster journey which results in increased benefits or speed to benefit. Third, learning from those who have already been successful increases the odds of success. But to what end?

The goal is performance excellence that is sustainable. Sustainable both in that it endures AND that it doesn't take from one stakeholder to give to another: sustainable in that it systematically creates value for all the stakeholders. The goal is a world without trade-offs where all the stakeholders are happy.

Sustainable excellence is the creation of ever-increasing value for multiple stakeholders including investors, customers, employees, suppliers and partners, the community, and the natural environment. It is achieved through the [re]design of an organization's systems to create continuously improving high-performance results across a comprehensive scorecard that compare favorably to relevant comparisons while embedding those changes into the culture of the organization.

Sustainable in this context means that the change endures, and it does not take from one stakeholder at the expense of another. Instead, sustainable excellence is designed to meet the needs of all the stakeholders. Only then will you have the organization you really want and society needs.

1

FORCES FOR CHANGE

INTRODUCTION

Law of Inertia – *"A body at rest tends to stay at rest unless acted upon by a net force. And, a body in motion tends to stay in motion."*
—Sir Isaac Newton

Research and practice suggest that many change initiatives fail to achieve all the results originally envisioned. Given past experience, it might seem that the odds are against change-focused leaders. However, it doesn't need to be that way. Successful leaders of transformation use the forces of change to overcome the status quo and keep the organization moving toward a better future.

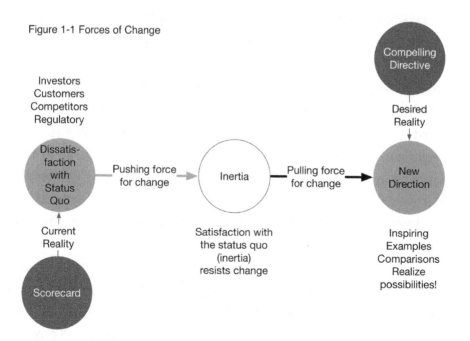

Figure 1-1 Forces of Change

There are two primary forces that have to be greater than the inertia or resistance to change (Figure 1-1). The level of dissatisfaction with the status quo combined with the power of a compelling vision of the future have to be greater than the inertia of the status quo. Organizations experience inertia in that if they are static, they tend to remain the same, and if they are dynamic they tend to continuously change and adapt. Those that change and adapt clearly have an easier time transforming and may not need a major transformation. However, many organizations are static and do not change much if at all — and then only when forced.

These three components — dissatisfaction with the current situation, a compelling desired reality, and resistance to change must be addressed by the organization architect in order to successfully [re]design and [re]build an organization or part of an organization (individual system).

DISSATISFACTION WITH THE STATUS QUO (PUSHING FORCES)

Dissatisfaction is a key factor in pushing people to change, but it is limited in that it does not provide any direction. In other words, unhappy people may not know what to do about it. For organizations that are not performing well, this can be what some have called a "burning platform." (Kotter, 1995) When the platform is burning, you know you need to get off so you don't get burned, but you don't know which direction you should jump.

Successful organizations, on the other hand, are often a little too satisfied with their performance and can become arrogant and complacent. Kotter and Heskett (1992) describe Xerox of the 1970s as an "extreme" example of this pattern. Xerox's lack of response to Japanese competition in the copier market resulted in a situation where in 1980 the Japanese were selling copiers in the United States for what it cost Xerox to make them (p. 77). This eventually led to a market share loss from 82% in 1976 to 41% in 1982 (p. 77). In fact, in some organizations, arrogance leads to a culture where negative feedback is not accepted and sometimes punished. Examples of the "Emperor has no clothes" are legion, including Napoleon. Napoleon's inability to accept feedback from his leadership team was a key reason for the tragic failure of his March to Moscow and the loss of over 380,000 lives (Kroll, Toombs, and Wright 2000).

There are many possible sources of dissatisfaction, including crises, parent organization pressure, competitive environment, and external regulatory pressures (e.g., accreditation, certi-fication). Many organizations simply are not performing as well as they would like. Some organizations face crises that are severe enough to drive them to change.

Crises

Crises are all too common and while some are caused by unforeseen external events, all too often the crisis is a result of complacency or arrogance. The sources of crises can range from financial insolvency to ethical violations. As one CEO who led a successful transformation described the situation at the beginning, "The company was in a lot of trouble. They never had made any money, had a lot of discrimination claims against the company for sexual harassment and age discrimination. Their customers didn't like them, and they had negative net worth, so it was in a tough situation."

There are many ways to react to a crisis. You can try to cover it up and deny the problem. You can try quick fixes to treat the symptoms. Or you can change the underlying systems and not only alleviate the current symptoms but prevent future problems.

Of course, the first task is to put out the fire. However, putting out the fire only stops the damage — it doesn't improve the organization. Once the fire is out, the next question is how to leverage the crisis to make the changes necessary to prevent the same type of crisis from occurring in the future. The answers to preventing problems in the future are found in the remainder of this book.

Stakeholder Pressure

In addition to the occasional crisis, stakeholders can put pressure on the organization to change. Stakeholders can be organized into six major categories: workforce, customers, investors, suppliers and partners, the community, and the natural environment. Pressure can come from an individual stakeholder group or a combination of stakeholder groups. Sometimes stakeholders have direct ways to apply pressure, including purchase power and social media. Other times, stakeholders find their voice in other governing bodies that represent their interests.

For example, the board of directors for a for-profit company represents the interests of the investors, although their responsibilities have been expanded to include other stakeholders such as the public. In addition, government legislatures and regulatory agencies put pressure on organizations through laws and regulations that are designed to protect one or more stakeholder groups including the public, consumers, investors, and so forth. The results from the comprehensive scorecard — including performance related to the six stakeholder groups — can also create dissatisfaction when compared to the desired level of performance or relevant comparison to organization and competitors.

Competition

While we can sometimes temporarily survive while ignoring stakeholder demands that are escalating, the situation can become untenable when competitors are more than willing to meet the stakeholders' demands. Opportunities abound for competitors in a rapidly changing environment with ever-increasing stakeholder demands and technology advances and disruptions.

When this situation reaches the extreme, it can become a crisis. In many cases, entire industries are shifting or, to put it euphemistically, been "disrupted." For example, Skype and other internet-based communication solutions have disrupted the telecom business without owning any traditional telecom assets. Many traditional universities have added online courses to their programs to meet the needs of students and the competition from non-traditional, for-profit online universities. How education will change is yet to be determined, but it is undergoing significant change in both delivery and financing. Changes are happening in all kinds of industries, and competition leveraging technology changes is helping drive much of that change. Unfortunately, some leaders decide to ignore the problem until it become a crisis.

Denial

Over the years I have noticed that high-performing organizations often have more "problems" than low-performing organizations. At first glance, this might not make sense. It didn't to me, anyway. After digging deeper into this phenomenon, I realized that the high-performing organizations didn't actually have more problems: they just recognized the problems that they did have. Low-performing organizations, on the other hand, actually had more problems, but they were either ignorant of those problems or in denial and didn't recognize their problems.

If you don't recognize your problems, then you can't work on them and improve. Consequently, organizations that don't think they have problems, but actually do, are lower performing than organizations that recognize their problems and work to address them. While denial is a common human behavior, it is a self-destructive approach to business (and life, but that's another book).

Predictable Cycle

Denial is a common first reaction to negative feedback. But if you stay in a state of denial, the problem is never addressed and usually gets worse. High-performing organizations have leaders who systematically work through their emotions and eventually accept the bad news and fix the problem.

When we get feedback that says we are not as good as we think we are, we often experience a predictable sequence of emotions. Our first reaction is often, "This can't be true." We deny the validity of the feedback, the credibility of the messenger, or both. If the messenger persists, we get angry and sometime fight back. If that doesn't work, then we try to bargain. If it won't go away, then maybe we can reduce the pain by accepting part of the feedback, but not all. If that doesn't work, we eventually get depressed. It is only after we accept the situation for what it is that we actually make progress toward improving.

This is similar to Elisabeth Kubler-Ross' grieving cycle

which consists of the five stages of denial, anger, bargaining, depression, and acceptance. I see this predictable sequence in myself, family, friends, students, and yes . . . leaders at ALL levels. What we are grieving is the loss of the idealized picture we all have of ourselves prior to the feedback. It is important to understand this cycle, anticipate this reaction, and develop a healthy way to move forward.

Creating Dissatisfaction

How can you increase the level of dissatisfaction with the status quo in an organization before you lose market share? In other words, how can you prevent the "burning platform"?

If you or your people are not dissatisfied, then you can create that dissatisfaction — and you should. It may sound crazy, but your future success depends on a certain level of dissatisfaction with the status quo. In the words of baseball legend Casey Stengel,

> *"If we're going to win the pennant, we've got to start thinking we're not as good as we think we are."*

There are at least three techniques that are proven to generate useful dissatisfaction: feedback from stakeholders, comparison of performance results to others, and organization assessments. One CEO in our study compared his organization to those in case studies and concluded, "In each case study, I saw our company versus the competition, and I came back with the view that we were not going to make it. I came back as a maniac really saying we were going to have to dramatically change."

If stakeholders are not proactively telling you how well your organization is doing, then you may have to seek out their input. Feedback from stakeholders can increase dissatisfaction if the feedback is accepted as credible and thought of as a gift as opposed to a nuisance. Comparison of your organization's performance relative to other organizations is a good way to understand what is possible and where your organization stands relative to their level. Comparison can create dissatisfaction and at the same time inspire improvement. Finally, assessment using a model or standard is another way to identify opportunities for improvement that might not emerge from comparison to others or feedback from stakeholders.

All three approaches to creating dissatisfaction are included in the leadership system (Chapters 2 through 10). However, the dissatisfaction and pushing forces are only half the force that is needed to overcome inertia.

DESIRED REALITY (PULLING FORCES)

While pushing forces are useful, many leaders of high-performing organizations seem to have a built-in desire to always improve. In other words, it is simply in their DNA to improve their methods and performance.

It is one thing for the leader to have this desire to improve and quite another to effectively enlist the help of organization members to create that improvement. Leaders use a variety of mechanisms including visions of the future and specific goals or objectives to communicate this desire to improve to the organization members. While dissatisfaction with the status quo PUSHES the organization to change, a compelling vision of a new reality PULLS people to change and provides direction for the change.

Vision

A vision is a picture of the ideal future state of your organization, including information system, supply chain, employee satisfaction, and so on. The three content components of the ideal organization vision are product or service, culture, and people. A vision should provide a picture of the ideal products and services or the value that the organization will create for the world. Ideally, a vision also provides a description of the desired culture as expressed in values, norms, symbols, etc. Finally, a vision should also include the individuals in the organization — what it is like to work for the company?

According to Belasco (1990) successful visions meet three criteria — they are timeless, inspirational, and provide clear guidelines for decision-making (p. 99). Covey (1989) proposed that everything is created twice: first in the mind, then in the physical world. To create your vision in the physical world, you need a well-thought-out, flexible plan to guide your efforts.

Practical Plan for Change

It is one thing to know that you are dissatisfied with the way things currently are and have a dream of a better world; it is quite another to know what to do about it. It is seldom that we know all the required steps to accomplish a transformation in advance, but it is important to know what the first steps will be. A high-level project plan with the major activities, deliverables, and benefits can help increase the motivation to change. The tension created by dissatisfaction and the compelling vision can create paralysis if there is not a credible path to actually achieve the new vision. Beckhard and Harris (1987) call this the "practicality of the change."

Many of the specific steps will be figured out along the way as the iterative path unfolds. These first steps vary depending on whether the situation is an organization transformation or simply a new management system such as an Enterprise Resource Planning (ERP) system or a new training program.

Follow Up and Follow Through

Finally, while priorities and clear objectives at the top are critical to successful change, the initiatives that support these objectives must be a priority on the agendas of regularly scheduled and frequent senior management forums to ensure actual implementation. A management review process is a formal follow-through process that provides for senior executive review and revision of key initiatives to keep the transformation on track and ensure that it is achieving the desired results. In the end, this package (content and process) of priorities, initiatives, and management review and refinement all have to make sense in order to be believable. If it is not believable, it will not generate enough motivating force to overcome the inertia or resistance to change. The development and deployment of strategy are key components in a larger leadership system. However, the best-laid plans will not result in change if leadership is not credible. The vision and practical plan must form a believable package that is supported by credible leadership — words and deeds.

BELIEVABILITY

The combination of dissatisfaction with the status quo, a compelling vision, and the practical plan of action must be believable to create sufficient force to overcome the inertia that resists change. As one CEO noted, "If you keep them too comfortable they're not going to move forward, but if you challenge them to the point that it's over the head, they get discouraged drop out. So it is a very delicate balance." There are three key elements to believability or credibility: (a) alignment and integration, (b) sustainability, and (c) logic (cause-and-effect).

First, alignment and integration determine the degree to which the dissatisfaction, vision, and the practical plan are consistent and working together. There are four key elements that must be aligned and integrated in order for any major change effort to succeed: stakeholder needs, strategy (goals and objectives), the action plans along with resources (systems), and the performance measures (scorecard).

Second, sustainability is the degree to which the change will actually become institutionalized and remain effective in the future. Sustainability has several components but one of the most important is the degree to which the changes produce value for multiple stakeholders. If one or more of the key stakeholder groups is short changed by the changes, then they will work against the change and undermine your efforts.

Third, logic (Action = Results) is the degree to which the actions or first steps make sense given the gap between dissatisfaction and vision. This requires a "systems perspective" of the organization. A system perspective includes an understanding of the cause-and-effect relationships within the organization. For example, an organization might determine that an investment in customer service employee training will result in improved customer service which, in turn, will result in repeat business and referrals and ultimately increased revenue. However, even the most credible plans encounter resistance.

RESISTANCES TO CHANGE

The combined pressure from dissatisfaction with the status quo (pushing force) and the compelling vision (pulling force) must combine and be greater than the resistance to change (inertia). In addition to creating and maintaining tension for change, leaders of change have to deal with resistance. Few people like change, but we tend to like change that is imposed on us the least. One successful leader of transformation made the comment, "Change which I initiate is exciting, but the change that is forced on me is debilitating."

One way resistance can be reduced is through a collaborative approach that involves the stakeholders in designing and implementing the change. The leadership style of the CEOs in our research was characterized by respect for all people and a collaborative approach to developing and deploying strategy, all of which helped to reduce the resistance to change. A collaborative approach helps reduce defensive routines while maintaining the pressure to change (Ford and Evans, 2006).

When all else fails one could use the technique of one CEO who said, "We are going to try it for a year. If it doesn't work, we will go back to what is NOT working now!" Successful leaders of organization transformation effectively address resistance to change.

DIAGNOSTIC

If you are dealing with a change initiative that has stalled, chances are one or more of the forces of change is the problem. For example, if you were running a non-profit charitable organization and were dissatisfied with the decreasing amount of donor contributions, what would you do?

To create a believable approach, you would first have to understand the donor's needs, wants, and desires and the nature of their dissatisfaction. Second, you would need to understand the donor's vision: what do they want to accomplish? Finally, you would need to determine how the organization should change to create significance for the donor. Every time I have used this approach to diagnose a stalled change initiative, one or more of the variables creating the tension for change was zero or near zero.

Reflection Questions

1. Take a moment to reflect on your own organization and situation. Begin with the **dissatisfaction**.

    What are you dissatisfied with in your organization?

    What are the sources of dissatisfaction?

    How dissatisfied are you with the current organization?

    How dissatisfied are the organization members?

2. Now take a moment to think about what success looks like for you and your organization.

    Do you have a compelling vision of how you would like it to be?

    What is pulling you to be better?

    Do you have a practical plan to make the vision a reality?

    Are the forces for change and the practical plan credible? If not, why not?

3. Now identify what is holding you back from moving forward.

Is the dissatisfaction and power of the vision enough for you to get off the couch and start improving the organization?

If not, what could you do to create more tension?

The forces for change are necessary to overcome the inertia of the status quo. The leader as organization architect must understand, create, and leverage these forces to effectively transform the organization. The next nine components (Chapters 2 through 10) form a leadership system that integrates the forces for change. These leadership activities apply the concepts of dissatisfaction with the current reality, the desired reality, planning, and credible leadership to move the organization toward sustainable excellence. The forces for change have to be managed throughout the transformation.

2

STAKEHOLDER VALUE

INTRODUCTION

"Never delegate understanding."
–Charles Eames

Have you ever been surprised by the announcement of a new organization policy? Have you ever thought, "What were they thinking?"

What did you say to your coworkers? What did you say to your boss? What did you do? Effective organization and management design depends on an in-depth understanding of the key stakeholders of the particular organization, system, process, or project being designed.

Understanding stakeholders' needs and desires is both the center of the Leadership System and the first step in the Design Framework (See Chapter 6). In many cases, if just a little more time were taken consulting key stakeholders as part of the design process, some of these surprises and missteps could be prevented or at least mitigated. Stakeholder value is the center of the leadership system because it informs and helps align the other eight components from vision and strategy to the scorecard and learning.

An underlying assumption of this framework is that sustainable excellence requires the creation of value for ALL key stakeholders. In other words, designing an organization that creates "win-win" solutions for all stakeholders vs. simply taking from one to serve another. In this context, there are at least six key stakeholder groups: customers, workforce, investors, suppliers and partners, society and community, and the natural environment.

SIX CORE STAKEHOLDER GROUPS

For any given organization, stakeholders can be organized into six groups (Figure 2-1). We address the needs of the customers, the workforce, suppliers and partners first because they create the value for the investors and represent the core of any successful business. Depending on the type of organization, the customers might be paying recipients of products and services, primary beneficiaries of non-profit or government services, patients, or students.

Modern workforces are composed of members from a variety of employment situations including, employees (full- and part-time), contractors, and non-profit volunteers. Inputs to the organization are provided by a variety of external organizations from suppliers of components and materials to partners that share both risk and reward. Investors provide the financial resources to make the value chain possible. For-profit investors include owners, stockholders, lenders, etc., and they expect some sort of monetary return on that investment. Non-profit donors provide resources to conduct the operations and serve the primary beneficiaries and they want the most impact for their donation. Taxpayers, like donors, fund the operations of the government and want the most benefits for the least tax burden. The public and local communities in which the organization operates are stakeholders in many aspects of organization operations. Finally, the natural environment and future generations find a voice in the other five stakeholders, public policy, and regulation. The six groups can be segmented into sub-categories based on their different needs, wants, and desires.

Figure 2-1 Six Stakeholder Groups

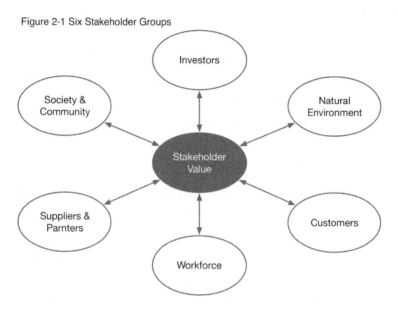

Customers

We begin with the customers because they are the group that the organization is (or should be) designed to serve. We bring people together and organize their efforts to design, build, and deliver products and services that individuals can't accomplish by themselves. For the commercial, profit-seeking organization, profit is a byproduct of doing that well.

While organizations serve many purposes in society, serving the customers is the main mission of the organization. In other words, without a customer to serve, there is no reason for the organization. Depending on the type of organization, the customers might be paying recipients of products and services, primary beneficiaries of non-profit or government services, patients, or students.

Customers of for-profit organizations typically exchange money for products and services. The relationship is often clear. Non-profit "customers" are the primary beneficiaries of the non-profit organization products and services. They often do not exchange any money with the organization, although there are exceptions and partial payments situations. Customers of non-profit organizations are the people who benefit from the output of the non-profit such as feeding hungry children, afterschool programs, etc.

While some government organizations consider the taxpayers customers, it is not generally helpful to identify taxpayers as customers. Taxpayers are the investors providing the resources, but they are not always the consumers or beneficiaries of every government program. While taxpayers and beneficiaries are often the same people, as a taxpayer they are investors and can't provide feedback on their needs if they are not the direct beneficiary of the service provided. Government "customers" like non-profits are the primary beneficiaries of the products and services. At the local level, those who use the roads that are built and maintained by government organizations and their contractors are the customers. At the national level, the overall population benefits from national security.

Many non-commercial organizations have difficulty viewing the people they serve as customers and instead choose other words to describe them such as clients, students, patients, so on and so forth. Part of the difficulty lies in a narrow view of customers as consumers of commercial goods and services. While identifying the customers for a profit-seeking retail business might be straightforward and easy, other situations are not so clear-cut.

Participation

Even for-profit companies have difficulty figuring out how to best serve customers when they participate in the production and delivery of the product or service. The degree to which the customer participates in the production of the product or service influences the company-customer relationship and the nature of the product or service. The degree of customer participation influences what you can control with respect to quality, outcomes, etc.

For example, a customer of the local health club is using a service but must participate in order to accomplish the desired results. The health club provides equipment and coaching, but the customer has to get on the treadmill and do the work to get the desired results. The health club can't control how much effort the customer puts into their workouts, how often they workout, or how much they eat and drink. So the health club can't guarantee the customer any results.

What the health club can control is the quality and serviceability of the equipment and the quality of coaching. So it is critical to define the product and service clearly and carefully while making the roles and responsibilities of each party clear. A similar situation exists in education.

Students as Customer

May educators that I have worked with resist the notion of students as customers. Part of their reluctance is due to the nature of the product and service (education) and the results that depend on the student's ability and effort. As mentioned previously, when educators think of a customer, they often think of the local retail-outlet customer. However, that is only one type of customer as noted in the for-profit health club example.

The first step is to define the education products and services. For colleges and universities, the product offering might be defined as "the opportunity for the customer (student) to earn an accredited degree." Like the health club, the university provides facilities (sometimes online), curriculum, and professors (coaches). Try as they might, the professors and administrators cannot control or guarantee that learning will take place. Nor can they guarantee successful completion of degree requirements. The student-customer must do the work to learn and earn the degree. This makes it difficult to determine how to improve, what to improve, and who needs to improve.

Patients as Customers

Like students, patients are involved in a process. While a surgeon might be able to control the process while you are sedated, the overall healthcare outcome is a combination of your behavior, prevention, previous interventions, heredity, and other factors. As with the gym or education, to be most effective, healthcare is a partnership between the provider and the patient. Your general practitioner doctor can provide accurate diagnostics, advice, and perform procedures. But YOU have to do the diet, exercise, and take your medicine when directed in order to achieve the desired results.

As in the health club and school, the patient is a participant in the delivery of healthcare and thus partially responsible for the results. In addition to their level of participation in the process, customers often do not actually understand what they need. However, customers are seldom a homogeneous group with the same needs, wants, and desires. Segmentation is based on the assumption that one size seldom fits all.

Segmentation

For similar products and services, customers often have differing needs, wants, desires, and objectives. Customer segmentation informs the design of the products, physical environment, placement, price, promotions, and the people, processes, productivity, and quality. Different customer segments often have differing reasons, requirements, and objectives for the product or service. For example, one segment might want high-performance, another segment might want status symbol, and another segment might want low cost. In addition, the environment is often an integral part of the customer experience from the ambiance of the coffee shop to the online interface. Different sub-groups might prefer to shop for the product in different places such as online vs. a shopping mall. Different segments often have different price points. For example, a business professional might pay more for the same product vs. a recreation buyer. For example, fewer people travel business class for vacation than do for reimbursed business travel.

The development of promotions, including messaging and media, is informed by specifics from the segments. Customers interact with the people and processes in the organization and different segments often have differing expectations for those interactions. In fact, the quality of the relationship is often as much or more influential in customer satisfaction as the quality of the product. This influences the design of the systems and culture of the organization. Finally, productivity and quality determine the value that is available to pass on to the customer. Value often has the largest influence on purchase decision.

There are two basic approaches to segmentation — individual consumer segmentation and organizations as customers (B2B) segmentation.

Individual Customers

We start with individual customers, including users and primary beneficiaries, who can be segmented using a wide variety of criteria. All too often, organizations segment customers based on the product type, but that is a company-centric approach. The goal here is to base the segmentation on the differences from a customer- or problem-centric approach.

There are often group characteristics that influence or predict their needs. Some of the typical customer segmentation options include geography, socio-economic factors, gender, education, profession, etc. In some instances, those segments are so numerous that we identify the key options and let the consumer select the best fit for themselves. Due to advances in technology, information, and communication, this kind of flexibility is possible for many products and services. Customer purchase decisions are often influenced by a variety of influencers including family, friends, experts, and social media articles and ratings. While it is sometimes difficult to identify or do anything about these influences for individual consumers, it is possible to identify and address the needs of these influencers in an organization.

Organizations as Customers

In addition to the types of segmentation used for individual customers, there are a few characteristics specific to Business to Business (B2B) or Organization to Organization (O2O) situations. There are at least three types of characteristics that are useful for segmentation of organizations: geography, the individual organization, and types of decision influencers.

With geography comes a list of characteristics that can be important to the marketing processes and products, such as country culture, laws and regulations, and economic conditions. Some organizations have a different segment for each country, and sometimes countries that are similar can be grouped into regions. Your specific situation will dictate the approach that is most useful. Organizations are often so large and have such distinctive needs that an individual organization might itself be a segment. This often occurs when dealing with large corporations or the government.

In addition to geography and the idiosyncrasies of individual organizations, there are often multiple people inside the organization with different needs and varying degrees of influence over the purchase and repurchase decisions. When an organization makes a purchase there are often multiple people involved with different agendas and priorities. The internal influencers can be grouped into three categories including users, administrators, and leaders (decision makers). The influence and involvement of each group varies depending on the product or service and the price. Users often make the decision for low-cost, front-line purchases while administrators (e.g., supervisors and purchasing) often are needed to approve certain higher cost purchases. For large, expensive purchase decisions, leaders are involved and often make the final decision based on advice from the users and administrators.

Boeing Aerospace Support, a 2003 Baldrige Award Recipient, segmented their customers based on three dimensions or tiers which they depict as a 3-D Cube (Spong and Collard, 2009, p. 27). Tier 1 was Geography — International or U.S. Tier 2 was the

Specific Organization (e.g., Air Force). Tier 3 were the Internal Influencers (Users, Gate Keepers) and Decision Makers. Spong and Collard describe the process where the senior leadership team developed their cube as "a defining moment" in their journey to excellence (pp. 27-28).

Profitability

Some organizations find it useful to segment customers by profitability. In an environment of limited resources, investments for improvement often have to be prioritized based on their expected economic return. Volume and price over time result in the lifetime value of the customer. When cost is considered, the profitability of specific customer segments can be determined. The more profitable a customer segment is, the more you can afford to add additional features and functions to their experience.

Some high-maintenance customer segments are difficult to serve profitably and thus can be poor investments. One example that many people are familiar with is the frequent flyer model that airlines use to segment their customers. Frequent flyer programs provide additional higher cost services to customers that produce more revenue and profit. They also are an attempt to encourage repeat business.

Customer's Customer

While it is critical to understand the immediate customer, in some situations it is important to understand the customer's customer. Why? Because the immediate customer doesn't always understand what they need in order to serve their ultimate customer. For example, when we treat students as customers they do not always know what they need to know to get and succeed at the job they want. Consequently, education providers also need to reach out to employers to understand what they need so they can build that into the education program. A similar situation exists for some component manufacturers (e.g., sound systems for cars).

The more we know about customers, the better solutions and offerings we can develop. Depending on the type of organization, the customers might be paying consumers of products and services, primary beneficiaries of non-profit or government services, patients, or students. It is not just a matter of semantics. Identifying the customers correctly is critical to designing the entire organization. We design from the outside in — from the customer to the production systems to the suppliers and partners. Customers of all types seem to have an insatiable appetite for better, faster, and cheaper. Their demands have extended into social responsibility issues and many now make product choices based on the impact on the natural environment. In the free market, competitors are always happy to help raise the bar.

Workforce

A talented and engaged workforce is critical to success today, tomorrow, and next year. Even during economic downturns and periods of high unemployment, the battle for the best talent is still a challenge for organizations. Unfortunately, according to Gallup, the evidence suggests that most organizations are losing that war as most employees are looking for other opportunities and are not engaged. While leaders often say people are their greatest asset, many leaders are attempting to maximize income and profit with only one third or less of the workforce engaged.

We need better ways to attract, engage, and retain talent. Understanding the different workforce segments and their individual needs should inform both the overall organization strategy and individual system designs. We segment stakeholders into sub-groups based on their different needs, wants, and desires. Our purpose is to understand their different needs so that we can design appropriate solutions to address those needs. Segmentation criteria can be organized into three groups: job type, demographics, and employment category.

Job Type

We begin with job type. This may be the most important factor as it informs the strategy, human resource development plans and activities, and support decisions. It seems obvious to point out that the needs of a front-line manufacturing worker assembling tractors will be different than a research scientist in a DNA lab. The nature of the job or work generally falls into four categories or segments including physical, information, creative, and bespoke. We discuss each type further in the section on the nature of the system in Chapter 6.

Each job type segment or category can be further segmented into more specific sub-segments based on the particular work and how it impacts the organization support system including training and development, work environment (e.g., safety), supervision, and reinforcement or inceptives. The specific job requirements compared to the employee's capabilities informs the needs assessment and subsequent training and development program design. In addition, the type of job influences the most effective motivation mechanisms and incentives.

Demographics

Within a given job type, worker needs vary based on a variety of characteristics including cultural background, education, generational cohort, and location. Cultural backgrounds can vary in the same office. This diversity in cultural norms and habits can create a diverse set of needs and desires. Education also drives the design of many organization policies and processes including the training and development programs. The differences in generational cohorts (e.g., Baby Boomers, Gen X, Y, and now Millennials) have been widely researched and discussed.

Finally, the location of the workers can create different challenges and needs. For example, workers located in New York City may have very different needs than those in a small town in the Western United States or virtual workers in Europe or Asia. While this used to be an issue for a few larger multi-national corporations, even some small business now have virtual assistants, specialists, and even manufacturing located around the world. In addition to job type and demographics, there is the nature of formal relationships with the organization.

Formal Relationships

Depending on the type of organization, the workforce stakeholders could be a combination of employees, volunteers, and contractors. The needs of each type of worker vary depending on the situation. Employees generally come in a couple of types including salaried, hourly, full- and part-time. Some employees may be represented by collective bargaining organizations and agreements. Employees both full- and part-time make up the workforce for most commercial, non-profit, and government organizations. This core group of employees is often supplemented by other types of workers including contractors.

Contract workforce has become more numerous over the last decade and includes a wide variety of situations from delivery truck owner-operators to large contractor firms that supply pseudo-employees to a customer firm. The needs of employees often differ from those of contractors and freelancers. Some non-profit organizations use volunteer labor to supplement their workforce. Volunteers offer many benefits as well as challenges for leaders. Each of these groups has their own characteristics and needs.

Government organizations can be even more complicated with a mix of employees, political appointees, elected officials, and contractors, each with different needs and expectations. The trick is to understand the segments that are specific to your unique situation and use the needs of those segments to inform the design of the organization, systems, policies, etc.

Suppliers and Partners

Inputs to the organization are provided from a variety of external organizations from suppliers of materials and components to partners that share both risk and reward. Suppliers and partners are more than just raw materials and component parts dropped off on the loading dock: suppliers are often integrated with the workforce. The more they are integrated into your processes, the more their needs are important inputs to the design of your operations. While their impact varies depending on the situation, supplier and partner performance influences your organization's performance. In other words, if you squeeze suppliers on price, they won't have the resources to improve their products and services to help you improve your business.

Depending on the situation, segmentation of suppliers is often similar to customer and workforce segmentation. In addition, sometimes there are situations where you may want to segment suppliers based on the cost and criticality of their input. I don't spend a lot of time managing my supplier interactions with the office supplies store down the street (nothing against my local office supplier). But I do spend a lot of time managing the relationships with graphic designers, website providers, etc. Some organizations have developed supplier segments based on the work they are doing and whether it is a core competency or not: in other words, whether it is a critical part of the business vs. a commodity. With the customer, workforce, and supplier/partner segments identified, the value-chain stakeholders are now complete. The remaining three stakeholder groups are the investors, society, and the natural environment.

Investors

Regardless of the type of organization — commercial, non-profit, or government —it costs money to operate the value chain. Investors come in a variety of shapes and sizes, depending on the situation and type of organization. For-profit investors provide capital and expect a monetary return on their investment. For-profit investors can be segmented into several categories, including owners (private and publicly traded stockholders) and lenders via a variety of financial vehicles.

Needs for each segment are different. Private (often family) owners of companies often have a longer-term perspective and are building an economic engine for the future. Publicly traded stock holders often have only a temporary (short-term) interest in the company. Lenders are interested in the very specific terms and conditions related to the particular financial instrument and the associated risks.

Non-profit investors (donors) provide capital to fund the activities (value chain) of the organization and they expect the most benefit to the primary beneficiaries of those non-profit services (e.g., hungry children). Non-profit donors want expenses to be low so more of their donor money goes to the primary beneficiaries. In many cases, they are increasingly interested in "helping" you manage the firm.

To assume all your donors have the same motives and requirements is a mistake. Often, non-profits have deeply held beliefs about their donors and what they want. While these beliefs may have been true at one point, they are often untested and out of date.

Government investors (a.k.a. taxpayers) provide capital and expect the best government services for the least amount of tax burden. The ability to understand and serve such a diverse group is limited by government processes. Depending on the type of government you have, taxpayers are represented by government officials (sometimes elected) who decide what is best for the taxpayers. However, once the mandate for the government agency is determined and funded, it is the responsibility of leaders to figure out how best to deliver the mandated services for the least tax burden. Taxpayers are also members of society and live in the communities where we operate.

While financial solvency and profit are the lifeblood of the organization, they are not the purpose of the organization. Extending this analogy further, our bodies require blood and oxygen to survive but that is not why our bodies exist.

Organizations require money to survive and thrive, but that is not their primary reason for existence.

In addition to the traditional investors, there are some situations where the person or organization paying for the products and services is not the user or customer of the product or service. For example, parents often pay for college but they are not the customer of that process. While it is true that they are a key stakeholder and want their children to get an education so they can get off of the "family payroll," they are more like an investor than a customer.

The point here is not about semantics. We classify stakeholders so that we can then use the information about their needs to design different aspects of the organization. In the case of parents we meet their needs if we meet the needs of the students and future employers for a reasonable cost or investment.

Society and Community

We allow businesses and non-profit organizations to exist and have specific legal status because they serve the economic needs of society. Organizations produce needed products and services, employ citizens, and buy from other organizations that employ citizens. Organizations and individuals then pay taxes to fund services essential for the organizations to operate and individuals to live. All types of organizations — commercial, non-profit, and governmental — create and exchange value. Regardless of legal status, they are all integrated into one economic system. Consequently, as the organization designs the products, services, and operations to make money or use the donated funds effectively, they also have a larger reason for existence, and that is their contribution to society and the local community.

While some organizations treat corporate social responsibility as a veneer layer or department separate from the other operations, creating value for the multiple stakeholders and avoiding trade-offs requires that it be integrated into all aspects of the organization. When we fail to proactively address the needs of society and our local communities, the citizens find a voice through other media. The citizens influence elected officials and government agencies who then create policies and regulations to address their needs.

In addition, everyone with an internet connection can broadcast their experiences and opinions to the world via social media. Sometimes, third-party surrogate stakeholders represent the interests of citizens and consumers through accreditation and certification programs. Unfortunately, many of these methods are inefficient and set up an adversarial relationship.

High-performing organizations proactively address the needs of society and the local communities. See the discussion in the Introduction Chapter on "New Attitude" and Dr. Alexander's approach to addressing the needs of multiple stakeholders. Stakeholders often wear more than one hat — your customers are also members of the community, employees, or even employers too.

Natural Environment

The natural environment doesn't have its own voice. Instead, the natural environment finds a voice and influence through the other five stakeholder groups. For example, there is a growing number of consumers who will pay a premium for environmentally friendly products and services from firms that are good corporate citizens. If you can figure out how to provide environmentally friendly products and services for a comparable price, that could be a competitive advantage. The most talented workers have options and are increasingly choosing to work for organizations that are good corporate citizens, and that includes being environmentally friendly.

A major accounting firm executive told me that the #1 question asked by potential hires in the interview process is about their social responsibility values and goals. This influence is moving up and down the supply chain. Investors are recognizing the risks associated with poor environmental practices and making investment decisions accordingly. Society is putting pressure on organizations to improve their environmental performance using government regulation and social media.

One way to organize the requirements is to segment the natural environment into categories including air, land, water, and energy. Then the direct linkages to the value chain can be examined including the sources, inputs (materials), use, and recycling. All too often the reluctance is based on the notion that we have to give something up to be environmentally friendly. While that might sometimes be required, it is often a false choice.

SYSTEMS PERSPECTIVE

All six stakeholder groups have needs and demands, putting increasing pressure on leaders to figure out how to create value for all of them at the same time. When you step back and look at all six stakeholder groups together, it can seem a bit overwhelming. If we view these requirements through the lens of the current system, the only solution might be compromise and trade-offs. In other words, take something from one stakeholder to serve another.

The only way around this is to redesign the systems with a new attitude and a systems perspective. Once you adopt a systems view, it becomes clear that there is a business logic of value exchanges between the stakeholders. In fact, there are plenty of examples of where it is possible to make even more money serving the multiple stakeholders including the environment. (e.g., Anderson, 1998). The task is to move beyond individual stakeholder needs to a true system of service.

System of Service

The core concept is that stakeholders are interconnected, making it not only possible to create value for all of them, but also the only way to sustain high performance (Figure 2-2). There is an old saying in business, "You better be serving the customer or serving someone who is."

We begin with a highly talented and motivated workforce that creates great products, services, and experiences for customers. Customers are delighted and come back, spending more money, referring friends, and growing the top line. Investors are happy as the revenue grows and operational improvements result in greater efficiencies. This flow is enhanced even further by high-performing suppliers and partners who provide great input into the value chain, earning repeat and referral business, resulting in the capital to continuously improve their products, services, and operations. When all this is done in a way that is ethical and provides value for society and the environment, we are able to attract talented workers, consumers who care, and investors concerned about risk. All of the above provide even better

financial performance, benefiting the investors and the other stakeholders through profit sharing and improved products, services, and operations.

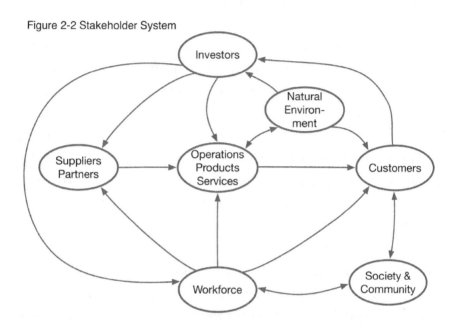

Figure 2-2 Stakeholder System

I once worked for a company where the CEO used to tell employees NOT to focus on the financials. In fact, the company didn't have financial goals, at least none that they communicated to the workforce. The CEO would often use basketball to explain how we grew the business and made even more money. He said, "Watching the financials is like playing basketball while watching the scoreboard."

You don't put many baskets through the hoop (customers) while watching the scoreboard (financials). You put balls through the customer hoop by working effectively as a team and focusing on customer needs. If you do that well, the scoreboard will change in our favor. He understood how the system of business worked and used that to focus the workforce on the things that mattered most to the long-term success for all the stakeholders.

Challenge of Systems Thinking

Given that there is over 50 years of research and application of the concepts of systems, you might be asking, "Why don't more leaders take a systems approach?" "Why didn't I learn about this in school?"

There are two basic challenges to taking a systems approach and both have to do with human learning. First, it can be difficult for humans to grasp and learn how the system works due to the distance in time and space between actions and results. When you have immediate feedback, learning is relatively easy and quick. When there is a delay between actions and the results, learning is more difficult. In organizations, the results can take months and sometimes longer to show up, making it difficult to understand how a strategic decision last year is affecting performance a year later.

The second issue is we teach business function by function. Business schools are typically organized into silos for each functional area such as finance, accounting, marketing, management, etc. And then we wonder why graduates create functional silos in organizations. While many business schools include a capstone strategy course in an attempt to bring it all together, it is typically too little too late. The solution is to start now with the stakeholders and build systems thinking into the organization.

UNDERSTANDING NEEDS

The systems perspective requires that we understand the

stakeholders needs and their particular place in the system. The menu of methods to understand stakeholder needs can be organized into three categories: stakeholder perceptions, stakeholder behavior, and empathy profiles.

The most common methods for gathering stakeholder needs, desires, and preferences is to ask them directly using written and verbal surveys and focus groups. In addition, some organizations gather comments and feedback through interactions with the stakeholders. While stakeholder perceptions are useful, their actual behavior (e.g., purchase decisions) can provide even better insights. Finally, empathy profiles are used to understand stakeholder experiences and how those influence what they think and feel — and ultimately what they say and do. Each method provides different information, and when combined, can help develop a stakeholder profile.

Surveys and Focus Groups

One way to understand the stakeholders' needs and desires is to ask them. Two common methods are surveys and focus groups, each with their own advantages and disadvantages. Surveys typically ask quantitative, deductive questions to help validate requirements and discover additional preferences using a limited set of options. Surveys can also ask open-ended qualitative questions to gather information that can be used inductively to develop requirements.

It might seem obvious, but surveys can only gather information that they ask for. Focus groups are useful for going deeper into stakeholder experiences. Focus groups have the advantage of exploring previously unidentified issues. Both surveys and focus groups assume participants actually understand their own preferences. Other listening opportunities include interactions and unsolicited feedback during customer service exchanges and formal complaints. High-performing organizations use systematic approaches to capture their impressions from stakeholder interactions and informal feedback gains during conversation (including instant message conversations) with customers.

Another source of stakeholder feedback is social media. This might be one of the best unvarnished sources of what stakeholders are really thinking — at least the ones motivated to spend the time to share on social media, who may be your biggest fans and most dissatisfied stakeholders. While all these methods can provide useful information, they are limited.

Customers Don't Always Know What They Need

The first problem with asking customers is they are often unfairly influenced by the person giving them the survey. How many times have you been given a survey and the person then coached you on how they wanted you to answer the questions so that they could get a good rating and a raise or bonus? Even the best survey instruments can produce invalid information if the process is implemented by those who are being rated. Don't waste your money. And don't put your employees in a position to BEG for high ratings from their customers. If you want the best data, consider using third party anonymous surveys.

On the surface, it might seem arrogant and dangerous to say the stakeholder doesn't always know what they want. And it is, so we will be careful and clarify the nuances. Customers often know what specific problem they need to solve. For example, they need safe, quick, and economical transportation from one country to another. However, many to most airline customers (passengers) do not know what it takes to produce a safe, fast, and economical flight. They cannot help us define all the requirements of safety. Only airline professionals can do that. What customers can provide is their perspectives and experiences to help us use our technical knowledge to develop better passenger experiences.

Education has a similar challenge with students as customers. Student customers often do not know what they need to be successful in the career they are preparing to pursue. That limits their ability to tell us what they need with regard to knowledge, skills, and abilities for their profession. They can tell us what is working and not working regarding the content, media, or teaching. However, the student's effort and capability can be the problem, rather than the content, media, or teaching. So treating students as customers is not nearly as straightforward as some other customer situations. See the previous discussion in this Chapter on customer participation in the production process.

While faculty steeped in the profession often know much of what they need to teach, faculty are sometimes limited in practical experience, especially current challenges in practice. To fill the gap, some high-performing universities and colleges gather input from the customer's customer: in this case, the organizations that hire the graduates. Note: Requirements can also come from stakeholder surrogates such as the government via regulations, third party accreditation, certification programs, and activist groups. The solution to the issue of stakeholders not always knowing what they need is to gather and use multiple perspectives, including their actual behavior and decisions, to inform the design of the product, services, and delivery.

Behavior

Customers often tell us one thing on the survey and then do another when they make the decision to buy our product or service. There can be many reasons for this disconnect, including the survey problems identified in the previous section. However, even under the best circumstances, stakeholders may not understand the reasons behind their own decisions and actions. Actual behavior such as customer purchase patterns can tell us what customers really prefer.

One of the hardest things to know is stakeholder intentions. While we can ask stakeholders about their intentions, their actual behavior will confirm or disconfirm what they tell us. For example, we often ask our existing customers about their intent to buy from us again, renew subscriptions, etc. Their actual repeat business activity validates their stated intentions. The same is true for referrals. We can ask customers if they would recommend us to a friend, but unless we actually ask new customers how they discovered us, we will never know if they actually did recommend us. Stakeholder perceptions combined with their actual behavior provide a more complete picture of their needs.

Empathy Profile

While it is useful to ask stakeholders their perceptions and analyze their actual behavior, both approaches are limited in their ability to provide us with deeper insights into their behavior. Deeper insights into their thinking and behavior help us develop solutions that don't currently exist such as new products, services, and organization designs.

Empathy is the ability to understand and share the feelings, thoughts, and attitudes of another person. It is the key to creating value for multiple stakeholders. The empathy profile can help gain a deeper understanding of your stakeholders and what it is like to be them. An empathy map as described by Osterwalder and Pigneur (2010) is a visual technique for depicting what a person sees and hears, thinks and feels, and says and does — it also identifies their biggest pain points and potential gains. For our purposes as organization architects, we have modified the visual organization of the empathy map to include three sections each with two cells (Figure 2-3).

Figure 2-3 Empathy Profile Sequence

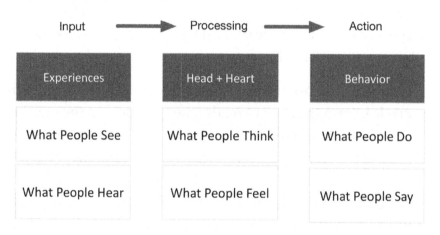

As we capture the data from the stakeholder interviews, surveys, and observations we can organize it around three phases: Input - Processing - Action. These involve what they HEAR and SEE (Input), what they THINK and FEEL (Processing), and what they then SAY and DO (Action).

This six-cell profile format helps you think about the connections and logic between the three major pieces: (a) what they hear and see or the input (organization, product, and service experience); (b) what they think or the processing that includes both rationale and emotional dimensions (head and heart); and (c) what they then say and do based on their thinking and feelings about their experiences (behavior).

To populate the cell in the framework, you need good questions. The usefulness of the completed empathy profile depends heavily on the quality of the questions. The questions should fit the context of the product or service, process or system, or organization.

ALIGN AND INTEGRATE

Segmentation of the stakeholder groups and identification of their needs inform the other eight leadership system components, including the other three cornerstones of strategy, systems, and scorecard.

Compelling Directive — Stakeholder segments and their needs inform the choices made when developing the mission and vision. You may decide to serve only a few or even one segment vs. trying to serve them all. For example, Monfort College of Business (2004 Baldrige Award recipient) decided at one point to eliminate all programs except the undergraduate business program, so they could be the best at one thing rather than good at many things.

Focused Strategy — Strategies are developed to address the unique needs, wants, and desires of the individual segments. While each segment might not have an individual strategy or specific goal, the strategies that are developed address the differing needs of different segments. Even when the product or service doesn't change, the marketing media and messages are often adjusted to communicate with the individual segments.

Enable, Empower, Engage — The various workforce segments and their specific needs inform the design and development of the plans, systems, and practices to enable, empower, and engage the workforce to accomplish the strategy.

[Re]Design Systems — The needs of the stakeholder segments inform the design of the systems, products, and processes. In addition, understanding the needs of the stakeholders is Step 1 in the system [re]design framework described in Chapter 6.

Comprehensive Scorecard — Segmentation is integrated into the design of the data collection, organization, and analysis in the comprehensive scorecard. Each stakeholder group and segment is measured. The specific needs of each stakeholder group/segment inform the development of predictor measures such as product and service quality. For a full description, see Chapter 7.

Org Performance Review - The stakeholder segments and needs combined with an understanding of the stakeholder system of service inform the analysis of the comprehensive scorecard results. In addition, the results of the review discussions inform the refinement of stakeholder segments and needs along with our understanding of the system.

Reinforce Behavior - Knowledge of stakeholder segments, needs, and inter-relationships informs what behaviors we need to reinforce as well as what types of reinforcement methods are effective for the workforce.

Learn and Improve - The stakeholder segments and system of service provide a framework for organizing the learning and improvement activities. In addition, lessons learned help to refine the stakeholder segments, needs, and our understanding of the interrelationships between the stakeholders.

LEADER AS ORGANIZATION ARCHITECT

Organization architect leaders set the example by treating stakeholders the way they want the rest of the organization to treat stakeholders. Leaders show respect for ALL stakeholders, which helps build positive relationships.

One way leaders build relationships is to involve stakeholders (and/or their input) in setting the direction for the organization and evaluating progress. This process includes leaders personally communicating (two-way dialogue) with stakeholders to gather information and share the direction and progress of the organization. Building relationships with stakeholders takes time. Leaders have to be persistent when it comes to building relationships with and creating value for multiple stakeholders regardless of the challenges.

Leaders develop relationships with stakeholders by spending time with them, developing a deeper understanding of their needs. Leaders understand the system and the connections between the requirements of the multiple stakeholders and creating ever-improving value for multiple stakeholders vs. a zero-sum game of trade-offs. Finally, leaders are continuously learning and developing new positive perspectives and approaches to meet and exceed stakeholder needs and desires.

Note: For an even more in-depth discussion on stakeholder theory see Freeman et al., (2010).

REFLECTION QUESTIONS

1. Take some time to identify your key stakeholder groups, segment, and their needs.

   Who are your key stakeholders and why?

   How do you segment (sub-groups) your stakeholder for each of the six types of stakeholders?

   What are the stakeholder needs and desires for each segment?

2. How do you identify and validate the needs and desires for each stakeholder segment?

   How do we systematically gain the data and insights needed to understand our stakeholders' needs and desires?

   How do we use stakeholder information to develop strategies to create value for our stakeholders?

   How does empathy for stakeholders inform our product, service, and operations improvement efforts?

3. How well are you doing today serving the needs of your key stakeholders?

   How satisfied are our investors (owners, donors, and taxpayers) with the value our organization creates for them?

   How satisfied are our customers (primary beneficiaries, students, patients) with the value our organization creates for them?

   How satisfied is your workforce (employees, contractors, volunteers) with the value our organization creates for them.

How satisfied are the leaders in my organization with our suppliers and partners' performance? How satisfied are our suppliers and partners with our organization?

How satisfied are our communities (public, society) with the value our organization creates for them?

How environmentally friendly are our products, services, and operations?

Creating an organization where all six stakeholder groups are satisfied is the central design challenge.

The focus on stakeholder needs and relationships helps provide a common alignment point for the strategy, systems, and scorecard. It is the cornerstone of cornerstones. It is the jumping off point for organization designs that create value for multiple stakeholders. Defining the organization you and your stakeholders really want and understanding the system of stakeholders informs the development of a compelling directive and strategy.

3

COMPELLING DIRECTIVE

INTRODUCTION

Where do we want to go and why? A compelling directive is the bridge between the needs of the stakeholders and the strategy to fulfill those needs. It is an important element for all organizations but is particularly important when embarking on an organization transformation. I first heard the term "compelling directive" from the CEO of an organization recognized as a Malcolm Baldrige National Quality Award Recipient. He used the term to combine the concepts of mission, vision, and values into a single touchstone for guiding the organization (Figure 3-1). Compelling directives come in a wide variety of shapes, sizes, and content, but the two most common components are the organization's mission and vision.

Figure 3-1 Compelling Directive

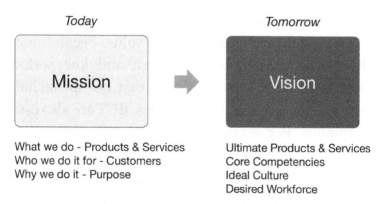

Although similar, a mission statement is distinct from a vision statement in purpose, style, criteria, and components. The mission and purpose focus on today and describe who the organization serves, what they do for them, critical processes, and a desired level of performance. The vision focuses on the future and empowers by providing clear decision-making criteria — it's also timeless. A comprehensive vision describes the "ultimate" organization products and services, culture including values, and the individuals.

You might be a bit cynical given that many organizations create formal mission and vision statements and hang them on the walls at the corporate headquarters, but then never actually use them to guide the organization. You might be asking yourself, "Do mission and vision statements really matter?"

Indeed, if the mission and vision statements are empty words on the walls at headquarters, then they are a waste of time, and worse, can cause cynicism among the workforce. In addition, some business researchers and writers have noted that both high- and low-performing organizations have mission and vision statements. This has led some to conclude that mission and vision statements don't matter.

There are two problems with this conclusion. First, the mere existence of mission and vision statements, regardless of quality and use, is not an indication of their value. Second, focusing on only the differences between high and low performers can result in a list of characteristics that do not include the elements that are common to both types, BUT are also essential to performance. For example, both high and low performing humans breathe oxygen and pump it through the blood. Both high and low performing humans must do this or there would be no performance at all. So focusing on those characteristics that are different can be useful but also dangerous and misleading.

Other research suggests that explicit mission and vision statements are important and useful to influence behavior.

For example, although he was originally skeptical, Mark Lipton's research showed ". . . that a clearly articulated vision, fully implemented across an organization, in fact makes a profoundly positive difference" (Lipton, 1996). Hodgetts, Kuratko, and Hornsby (1999) also found a vision of quality and how they would achieve it one of four characteristics common to Malcolm Baldrige Award recipients. In addition, our own research on Baldrige Award Recipient's supports the conclusion that mission and vision statements do matter. (Latham, 2013a).

Effective mission and vision statements compel the organization toward a better future. Regardless of their influence on transformation and performance, practice suggests that making the mission and vision explicit are useful intermediate steps between understanding the stakeholders and developing strategy. They're also useful tools for guiding consistent communication.

MISSION AND PURPOSE

The first question to answer is, "Why are we here?" As one CEO noted, "I think that people need a powerful purpose, and the leader has to be able to communicate that power. There is a purpose in what you're doing, and you've got to give people a reason for being. That's number one." To achieve sustainable excellence the generic answer to the mission question is: "to create value for multiple stakeholders." So the task here is to develop a specific answer for your organization.

"The mission statement identifies an organization's customers and critical processes, often with a qualifier of what level of performance the organization is dedicated to delivering" (Latham 1995, p. 66).

For existing organizations, the mission is already established, so you can identify the stakeholders and understand their needs before you examine the mission, vision, etc. For new organizations, the draft of your mission statement may come first, and the stakeholders are then identified based on that mission. Regardless of where you begin, it is often an iterative process that evolves over time. So while the mission and vision are relatively stable compared to other aspects of strategy, they are reviewed periodically and updated as needed. I suggest that you start from wherever makes the most sense for your organization's current situation.

You may be wondering, just what is the difference between the purpose of an organization and the mission of an organization? I wish there was a single, simple answer. While some have provided examples to illustrate this difference, there is little agreement on actual definitions that make the two distinct. For many organizations, the words are interchangeable and there is no difference. At least many organizations have not identified a separate and distinct purpose from the mission. However, for some organizations, the purpose the organization was created might be slightly different than their mission.

Some organizations differentiate mission (what they do) from purpose (why they do it). For example, some organizations describe their purpose as an innovative way to solve a problem for the customers or the outcome of the mission. In these cases, the purpose describes the impact on the customers. For example, the purpose (why they do it) of a small family-owned business might be to provide a long-term economic engine for the family and future generations. However, the mission (what they do) of the organization might be to design, develop, manufacture, and distribute farm equipment. Another organization's purpose

might be to make something easy or affordable. So if your mission includes WHY you exist then you probably don't need a separate purpose statement.

If your purpose statement includes what you do and who you do it for — the business you are in then you might not need a separate mission statement. If we focus on the key elements vs. the labels, we need the mission and purpose to identify three things: (a) what the organization does today, (b) who it does it for, and (c) why it does it. Ultimately, this is the benefit that the organization provides to the key stakeholders.

Bottom line: Purpose and mission can be separate descriptions, combined into one statement, and the label you put on it doesn't really matter.

VISION

What is leadership's ambition for the organization? What do the leaders of the organization want the organization to become? The task here is to describe the desired reality that provides the direction and the pulling force necessary to move the organization forward. While we have not been able to come up with a specific or universal formula for individual success, we have found that many successful people were able to picture themselves achieving their goals. This clear and often vivid vision of themselves in the future provided a guide to help them stay flexible but on the overall track as the actual journey unfolded.

This is particularly important when multiple people (e.g., the organization) are involved in a common journey. As one CEO said, "You can't take people to a place they can't see." An organization vision is a picture in your mind of the perfect organization — products and services, culture, and individuals. The three components of a comprehensive vision address the needs of the multiple stakeholders.

Three Key Components

The comprehensive vision includes descriptions of the future ideal products and services, culture, and individual development. While the mission describes what you do and for whom, the vision goes beyond today and provides a picture of the future. A vision provides a description of the ideal products and services or the value that the organization will create for the customers or primary beneficiaries.

How the organization serves its customers is influenced heavily by the culture of the organization. A complete vision includes a description of the ideal culture including the desired values. What are the desired values, behavior standards, culture norms, and philosophy of doing business? A vision also provides a description of the desired culture as expressed in the organization's heroes, symbols, and rituals that the organization would like to embody.

Finally, a vision addresses the value for the multiple stakeholders and what it is like for the individual internal and external stakeholders to interact with the organization. This is particularly important for the organization members (workforce). What does an organization that facilitates members reaching their full potential look like?

But does it matter if the organization's vision statement addresses all three components? That depends on how the vision is developed and used to influence decisions, strategies, and behavior in the organization — and how other documents address these three components. An effective vision statement is inspirational and provides a sense of purpose, is timeless, and provides decision-making criteria for all those instances not covered in the company policy manual that no one reads anyway. Ultimately, the compelling directive guides the organization's strategy (goals and objectives) which, in turn, direct all plans and activities toward a specific end.

Products and Services

How good do you want to be at the mission? If your vision is to be a LOW-COST provider, that will result in a different strategy and outcome than if you want to be the highest QUALITY provider. While sustainable excellence doesn't prescribe a particular strategy, it is based on high performance or excellence across a comprehensive scorecard. It is one thing to have a vision for the products and services and another thing to execute and achieve that vision. One exercise that has proven useful for organizations working to define their vision of the products and services is to identify their core competencies. According to Prahalad and Hamel (1990), core competencies are your organization's areas of greatest expertise that also provide a competitive advantage and are difficult for the competition to imitate. In other words, they provide a sustainable competitive advantage. For example, Honda makes many different types of vehicles but their competitive advantage is the design and manufacturing of great engines (Prahalad and Hamel, 1990). The core competencies can help provide an explicit connection between the product and service vision and the more specific strategy, including goals and objectives.

Culture

The creation and delivery of products and services is dependent on a supporting culture. Culture is a key element holding the four cornerstones of stakeholders, strategy, systems, and scorecard together. The key task here is to align the culture with the vision for the products and services and mission of the organization. We dig deeper into the key elements of values, rituals, heroes, and symbols in Chapter 12: Culture of Service. For now, start with identifying the most important values of the organization: those values that, when manifested, will support the vision for products and services and the mission.

While there is no single list of good values, here are a few examples from high performing organizations: leadership, integrity, quality, excellence, customer focus and satisfaction, teamwork, developing people, safe work environment, collaboration, accountability, diversity, engagement, corporate responsibility and citizenship, enhancing shareholder value, systems thinking, and innovation.

Values describe the underlying principles that provide a foundation for the desired culture. We can't directly see or measure values. Instead we infer the values of the organization or individual by what they do and the decisions they make. Choose your values wisely. What some refer to as "strong" cultures can become unbalanced and arrogant. When such a culture is successful, it can reinforce a narrow-minded view, which can become an impediment to learning and innovation. This is a recipe for decline as the world and competitors change. A strong team-oriented culture can create undesirable side-effects when the individual is lost in the process.

Individual

Ultimately, it is the behavior of individuals that creates both the organization culture and the products and services. At the core of success are individuals who are talented and motivated to contribute those talents to the mission and vision of the organization. The task here is to develop a vision of the organization where people reach their full potential and use those abilities to further the work of the organization in a "win-win" arrangement.

What is it like to work at the ideal version of your organization? Is your vision a workplace that inspires and enables workers to reach their full potential? This is not about the amenities in the playroom or volleyball courts, although those might be part of your vision. Humans thrive when they are challenged, have a compelling purpose, and the tools to meet that challenge and fulfill the purpose. These factors set the stage for developing the workforce portion of the strategy.

ALIGN AND INTEGRATE

The compelling directive translates stakeholder needs into the mission and purpose of the organization and the vision of the ideal organization, including products and services, culture, and individuals. The mission and vision inform the other eight leadership activities.

Stakeholder Value - Stakeholder segments and their needs inform the choices made when developing the compelling directive. The mission then identifies the specific customer stakeholders the organization serves. The vision describes the ideal organization for all the key stakeholders.

Focused Strategy - Mission and vision inform the strategy, which translates the compelling directive into specific goals and objectives. The strategy addresses both aspects of the compelling directive — the mission of today AND the vision for tomorrow.

Enable, Empower, Engage - The mission and vision provide timeless and inspirational guidance to enable and empower the workforce. The compelling directive provides clear decision-making criteria for those instances when the situation is not covered in the policy manual. The directive also helps to motivate people to achieve a purpose larger than themselves.

[Re]Design Systems - The mission and vision provide the overall picture of the ideal organization design and key design characteristics. It also guides organization [re]design decisions throughout the organization. The results from the [re]design initiative should contribute to the mission and achieving the vision.

Comprehensive Scorecard - The comprehensive scorecard includes measures (often indirect) of performance relative to the mission today and progress toward the vision for tomorrow.

Organization Performance Review - While the organization performance reviews focus on the stakeholders, strategy, and systems, the mission and vision provide a touchstone for decision-making and refinements to the plans and processes.

Reinforce Behavior - The compelling directive provides guidance on the type of behaviors that will support the mission of today and the vision for tomorrow. Included in the vision are the desired values, which are translated onto behaviors. Behaviors are then translated into the criteria for assessing and rewarding individual performance.

Learn and Improve - Learning and improvement support the mission today (what we do for stakeholders) and progress toward the vision for tomorrow. The vision includes all stakeholder segments. Learning and improvement also informs the refinement of the mission and vision.

LEADER AS ORGANIZATION ARCHITECT

The role of the leader with respect to the compelling directive varies depending on the level of the organization. Senior leaders are typically responsible for the development of the compelling directive. However, leaders at all levels are responsible for communicating and connecting organization members with the mission and vision. The development of a compelling directive is enhanced by collaboration with multiple stakeholders. This not only helps build relationships but also facilitates the communication and deployment of the mission and vision. Successful leaders of change are persistent in communicating and reinforcing the vision of the desired reality and culture change. A compelling directive that is focused on sustainable excellence focuses on the sustainable success of the entire organization system and all stakeholders. Full implementation throughout the organization requires that leaders engage people at all levels in discussion and translation of the compelling directive. The mission and vision are seldom static and leaders regularly reflect on and revise the compelling directive so that gives meaning and passion to people.

REFLECTION QUESTIONS

Take a few minutes to assess your mission and vision.

Is your current mission meaningful and does it pull the organization forward?

Is your vision inspirational and does it pull the organization to higher levels of performance?

Are your values explicit and do they pull the organization toward the vision of excellence?

Which key stakeholder groups does your mission and vision address?

A compelling vision combined with an understanding of the current reality (e.g., stakeholder feedback) creates tension and energy for change. At the same time, an effective mission, vision, and values are the basis for an empowered workforce — and essential for innovation and agility. In addition, an effective compelling directive provides guidelines for decision-making for all those situations not covered by the corporate policy manual. The compelling directive informs the focused strategy and helps leaders decide on the priorities AND maybe most important, it helps leaders say "No!" to those initiatives that are not essential to the mission and vision.

4

FOCUSED STRATEGY

INTRODUCTION

How will you accomplish the compelling directive? The mission and vision inform the strategy development process and the associated goals and objectives that, in turn, direct all plans and activities toward the vision. The tension created by the dissatisfaction with the status quo combined with the compelling vision can create paralysis if there is not a credible, understandable path to achieving the new vision. It is one thing to be dissatisfied with the way things currently are and have a dream of a better world; it is quite another to know what to do about it.

Everyone may want to create value for multiple stakeholders, but few organizations are successful. Most organizations work within the current system to allocate resources and make trade-offs between stakeholders. For example, they trade benefits for employees for less profit for investors. They assume a zero-sum game and view the world as a hierarchy. This limits them to an inferior menu of options such as low cost vs. differentiation and so on. This is a false choice. In order to develop a viable plan to accomplish the mission and vision of serving multiple stakeholders, you need curiosity, a systems perspective, and some creativity. Together, those traits can help you transform the organization and its offerings.

Leading an organization transformation to achieve sustainable excellence is, at its core, a strategy development and deployment process. The job of strategy development is to translate the stakeholder needs and the compelling directive into a strategy with clear and actionable goals, objectives, and initiatives. A complete strategy addresses the customer and how you will compete, including products, channels, and relationships along with the value chain and support operations. Initially, the strategy is the bridge between the external environment and the offerings. Then the strategy translates these external requirements and offerings into goals and objective for the internal system of value chains and support processes. In addition, a strategy to achieve sustainable excellence addresses all six stakeholder groups.

A strategy for sustainable excellence answers two basic question. First, what is the strategy to serve the external customers and compete? Second, what is the strategy to develop the organization so that it can serve all the stakeholders AND compete? The design challenge is to figure out how to create an enduring system and culture of service.

In fact, the central design challenge is to develop a strategy that creates win-win arrangements for all six stakeholder groups. The designer of a strategy development process has to address several challenges, including creativity, complexity, and the amount of structure that is optimum for the task of strategy development.

First, we have yet to develop a strategy process where you can simply "turn the crank" and produce a viable strategy that will win in the marketplace or fulfill your mandate for a government organization. Second, the development of strategy is inherently a creative process and thus needs just enough structure to facilitate group creativity and no more. The basic strategy development process consists of input (information and data), analysis (external and internal), and output (goals, measures, initiatives, and sponsor) (Figure 4-1).

Figure 4-1 Strategy Development Process

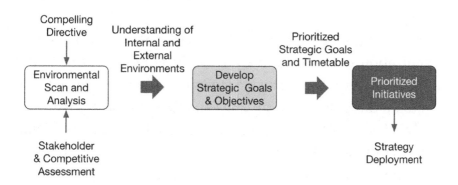

The design challenge is to develop the best questions for the strategy process to ask and the best sources of data and information, as well as the best formats, displays, and analysis methods to facilitate the development of the strategy.

INPUTS

While many for-profit strategy processes begin with an environmental scan focused on the market, a strategy to serve multiple stakeholders requires an expanded scan. The compelling directive (mission and vision) provides parameters to help focus the expanded scan. The mission and vision help reduce a potentially large task to one that provides the essential information to develop a strategy and associated goals focused on fulfilling the mission and progressing toward the vision. The needs for each stakeholder group and segment provide the foundation for setting performance standards. Performance relative to the stakeholder standards is measured by the scorecard and provides insights into the areas that need further improvement. Performance comparisons in the scorecard also help to clarify what is possible AND how well competitors are doing.

The results from organization performance reviews and organization assessments also provide insights into the potential internal changes that are needed to improve performance. There is often a direct connection between organization assessments and [re]design initiatives. Finally, additional economic, societal, and environmental scans are useful to complete the picture. Combined, these inputs inform a dialogue that produces a comprehensive sustainable excellence strategy that address the needs of multiple stakeholders.

ANALYSIS

There are a wide variety of tools, techniques, and technologies available to assist in the analysis of strategy inputs. A review of those methods is beyond the scope of this book. Instead we will focus on the key dimensions for analysis to produce the necessary outputs of a sustainable excellence strategy. Using the compelling directive as a lens to view the inputs, the stakeholder analysis begins with the external customers and competitive market. What are the opportunities and challenges? How will we compete? These are the central questions of strategy.

While non-profit and government organizations often compete for funding, how and how well they serve the external customers or primary beneficiaries is the central strategy question. Strategy for government organizations is often mandate-driven. They have a mandated and funded mission, so strategy is a process to determine how best to accomplish that mission. For-profit organizations, on the other hand, are opportunity-driven. They determine the mission and how they will chase market opportunities. Non-profits often occupy an intermediate position on the continuum from mandate to opportunity. The main external strategy is dependent on supporting internal strategies that will make the external strategy possible.

Value Chain

Once how the organization will compete or fulfill its mandated mission is determined, the analysis moves inside to the organization's value chain of products and services, operations, and suppliers and partners. The quality of the customer experiences, services, and products are determined by the design and execution of the value chain. Working backward, you should analyze the output of the value chain products and services first, then assess the design, development, and delivery of the products and services that create customer experiences. Next, analyze the performance of the operations and the key inputs from suppliers and partners that produce the products and services. Finally, analyze the performance of the support systems that enable the value chain components. What improvements are needed in order to achieve the overall strategy?

People and Culture

A value chain doesn't really exist without people working together to execute the processes. In other words, the people and culture bring the value chain to life. The analysis of the people and culture is focused on how well they support the value chain and in turn the overall strategy. What are the capabilities and capacity of the workforce? What is the current workforce performance? What are the norms and values of the culture? How do these support the value chain and the overall strategy? While the strategies, goals, and objectives are often different for the people and the culture, they are interrelated and support one another.

Society and Environment

Then the analysis focuses on the society and environmental challenges associated with the organization and its products and services. If you try to address all the economic, societal, and environmental issues that we face, it would be overwhelming. While we might be concerned with many of the big issues facing society, when it comes to our organization we only have influence on those aspects related to our products, services, and operations. Having a clear picture of our own organization first helps generate parameters or boundaries to work within. These boundaries help reduce the size and scope of the issues and allow us to work on those aspects that we can control or at least influence.

Some organizations have added society and the natural environment as "veneer" layers of initiatives to address specific issues. Corporate social responsibility (CSR) goals, initiatives, and programs help support the overall strategy and compelling directive. While this is progress, and many initiatives make significant contributions toward a sustainable enterprise, the next step is to fully integrate society and the natural environment into the strategy process. One option is to ask about the implications for society and the environment for all organization operations, products, and services. Here we briefly explore considerations for integrating the natural environment into the strategy.

There are three key areas to consider when integrating the natural environment into the strategy process: the sources of energy and materials, how they are used, and what waste is produced.

Options:

Change the energy and materials sources and supply chain

Change the value chain's energy and materials usage

Change the organization's energy and materials waste

These three categories of options are applicable across the value chain of the organization. Figure 4-2 identifies more specific options and consideration at the various stages of the value chain including supplies, logistics, operations, customers, employees, and investors.

Figure 4-2 Integrating the Natural Environment

Activity	Sources	Usage	Waste
Suppliers	Change design of supplier facilities and processes and sources of raw materials to use more renewable sources.	Change design of supplier facilities and processes and sources of raw materials to use less energy and materials.	Reduce the amount of energy and materials waste.Increase the amount of recycling.
Logistics	Change transportation modes to use more renewable sources.	Change design of packaging and transportation modes to use less energy and materials.	Reduce the amount of energy used for transportation and storage of supplies and materials
Operations	Change design of facilities and processes to use more renewable sources.	Change design of facilities and processes to use less energy and materials.	Reduce the amount of energy and materials waste.Increase the amount of recycling.
Customers	Change design of products and services to use more renewable sources.	Change design of products and services to use less energy and materials.	Reduce the amount of energy and materials waste.Increase the amount of recycling.
Employees	Engaged in alternative energy and materials projects	Increase the usage of low energy practices (virtual meetings and work). Engaged in energy savings projects.	Engaged in waste reduction and recycling projects.
Investors	Financial impact of alternative energy and materials sources.	Financial impact of reduced energy and materials usage.	Financial impact of reduced waste and recycling.

Integrating the options into the strategy development process can help identify goals, objectives, and initiatives to address the areas of greatest impact and return on investment. All too often, we identify many more opportunities for improvement than we have resources to address in a particular strategy cycle.

OUTPUTS

Seldom do we know in advance all the steps required to accomplish a transformation, but it is important to have a good idea what the first steps will be. Many of the specific steps will be figured out along the way as the iterative path unfolds.

Building on the compelling directive, the basic strategy is composed of four key elements (Figure 4-3).

Figure 4-3 Strategy Outputs

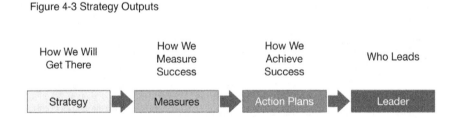

1. **Goals and Objectives** - The specific path we are taking to the mission and vision. The strategy described by the externally and internally focused goals and objectives.

2. **Measures** - How we will know when we are making progress and when we get there. Measures of progress and performance related to long- and short-term targets.

3. **Action Plans** - How we will achieve the necessary milestones toward the vision, including strategic initiatives and projects.

4. **Sponsors** - Who will sponsor goal and lead the initiatives. Each goal and associated initiative has an identified leader who is responsible for the overall initiative.

These four components directly or indirectly address the mission and vision as well as the needs of the stakeholders.

Goals and Objectives

Strategy development is a complex dialogue that includes a variety of inputs from the stakeholders, the compelling directive, the current performance, the external competitive environment, and the unique context of the organization. How the organization will achieve the mission and vision is described in the goals and objectives that address both the external market-driven products and services and the internal system-building capabilities to provide those products and services. Goals and objectives are the first output in the development of a comprehensive strategy.

Goals come in a variety of time horizons from less than a year to several years. The time horizon that makes sense for the organization will vary depending on the particular context. Some organizations such as aerospace companies plan out strategic goals ten or more years into the future, then create intermediate or short-term goals that provide a path to the longer-term strategy. Other organizations such as high tech computer firms may realistically only plan out five years with 18 month plans and goals for each product. To be effective, the goals need to provide the information in a way that is measurable, actionable, and manageable.

System of Goals and Objectives

The collection of goals and objectives is not a strategy unless they collectively describe the way the organization will compete and how they organization will be developed to compete. A visual depiction of the interrelationships of the goals and objectives helps leaders not only describe the logic behind the strategy, it also helps the leaders develop the strategy and identify the goals and objectives (Figure 4-4).

Figure 4-4 Strategy System Framework

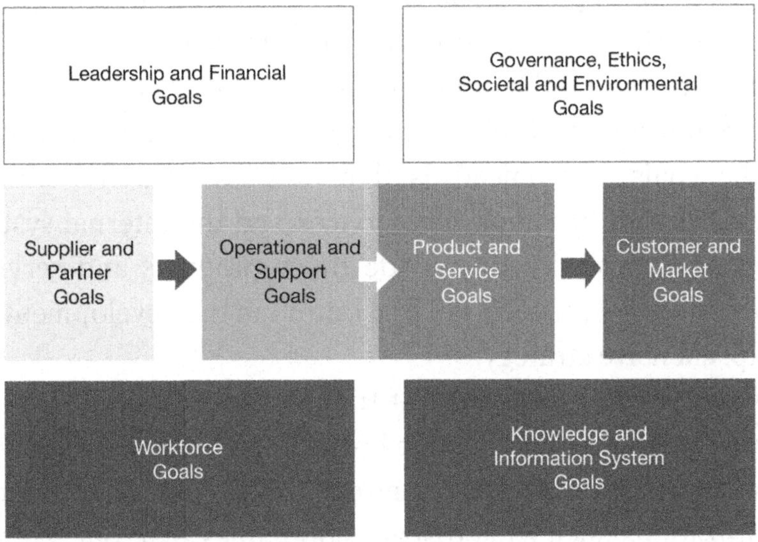

The idea of a visual depiction can be traced back to Kaplan and Norton's concept of a strategy map (Kaplan and Norton, 1996). Once the strategy logic is developed the goals need to be developed so that they are measurable, actionable, and manageable.

Goal Characteristics

Goals must be measurable, actionable, and manageable. First, goals have to be specific enough to provide a clear and tangible definition of success for the measures and the action plans. The longer the time horizon the less specific and predictable the goals.

Short-term goals should be very specific. Goals have to be measurable, otherwise we will not be able to track our progress toward the desired performance. Measures also allow us to compare performance with other relevant comparisons including competitors. Goals must be written in a way that can be translated into specific action plans with clear and specific deliverables. The goals must be clear enough to provide a basis for a "[re]design brief" for each strategic initiative. Be honest when answering the question, "Is the goal doable?" If the goal is unrealistic, people justifiably won't believe they can accomplish it.

Finally, a specific time is identified for the completion of the goals and objectives. This provides a basis for management and tracking progress.

Measures and Targets

How the organization measures success includes both organization performance and progress toward the strategy measures that connect the systems and the strategy. Performance metrics address the key organization performance metrics related to the particular goals and objective. The measures and results that informed the analysis that led to the goal are often the natural selection for goal measures. The measures allow for a quantitative definition of the goal by predicting a specific level of performance as a target to aim at when developing the specific initiatives. For example, a 10% increase in sales based on total revenue from sales or 90% of customers rate overall service in top two boxes on the customer satisfaction survey. This could be expressed as a change or improvement from 80 to 90% top two boxes.

Targets are tied to a specific time period (e.g., 5 years, 1 year, 90 days). For longer-term goals such as three to five years, intermediate targets (e.g., 90 days, 1 year) are often set to help track progress as the initiative unfolds. Typically, both short- and long-term targets are set based on the details of the project plans and resources committed to the project. So while initial measures and targets are identified after the goals are developed, it is an iterative process and these targets are refined once the initiatives are developed, prioritized, and selected.

Initiatives

How the organization will achieve the strategic goals, objectives, and performance targets is described in proposals for the key initiatives and projects. Unfortunately, leaders often have ambitions and expectations that exceed their capacity to execute. Developing proposals for the potential strategic initiatives is one method to help evaluate the details, impact, cost, and risks associated with achieving the specific goals. When proposals are developed using a standard template they can be compared and prioritized. A complete proposal consists of five sections that describe the project, identify the scope, deliverables, roles and responsibilities and an evaluation of the initiative. Initiatives are then compared and the portfolio is selected based on the impact to strategy, financial cost and benefit, and risk. Note:

This is a suggested proposal format and a starting point. Take it and modify it to make it fit your unique situation.

1. Description and Objectives

The first section of the strategic initiative proposal is a brief description with some key identifying information. This section sets the stage and provides a quick overview to help people understand what this initiative is about and how it's intended to contribute to the strategy.

1. Project Title: A short but distinctive title.

2. Point of Contact: Name of the person with overall responsibility for the initiative. This could be the sponsor but is more likely the project manager.

3. Description: A short description of the project that briefly describes who, what, where, when, why and how.

4. Strategic Goal(s) and Objective(s): Describes the explicit and clear link to the strategic objectives.

2. Scope

The second section goes further with details on what the project IS and IS NOT. In addition, the overall scope of the project is defined.

1. The Project Is: What IS included in the project.

2. The Project Is Not: What is NOT included in the project.

3. Functional and Departmental Scope: Identify the functions,

departments, divisions, etc. that are involved in or impacted by the project.

4. Regional Scope: Identify the geographic locations involved (as applicable).

5. The Project is Dependent Upon Other Projects and Initiatives: Identify the other projects that are ongoing that must be successful in order for this project to be successful.

6. Project(s) and Initiatives Dependent on This One: Identify the other projects that are dependent on the success of this project.

These details provide a foundation to identify the deliverables and key tasks.

3. Deliverables, Tasks and Schedule

This section identifies the key deliverables and major tasks required to complete this initiative. For each deliverable or task, develop five elements including:

1. Description

2. Dependencies between tasks and deliverables

3. Amount of work for that task

4. People required

5. Completion date

To encourage steady progress, major milestones should be within 90 days of the previous milestone. The deliverables and key tasks provide a basis to determine an estimate of the resources needed.

4. Roles, Responsibilities and Resources

Section 4 identifies how many people and how much of their time is required to successfully complete this project.

1. Project Lead: Identify the roles and responsibilities of the project leader(s). The more detail that is included in the description, the more accurate the workload estimate. As part of that description, estimate how much time this project will require (workload). If you estimate times in the full-time equivalent (FTE) format, it will make it easier to compare. For example, if the leader will need to spend on average 30% of his or her time on the project, then that is a .3 FTE.

2. Core Team Members: Most strategic initiatives require multiple disciplines and talents to accomplish. They often cross many parts of the organization. The core team member requirements are identified by describing the roles and responsibilities of the individuals needed. The workload is estimated for each using the FTE method above.

3. Operating Expenses: What are the operating expenses required to accomplish the initiative? Operating expenses include internal labor, consulting, travel, user training, maintenance, etc.

4. Capital Expenses: What capital expenses are required to accomplish the initiative? Capital expenses include equipment, software, etc.

5. Evaluate

The last section in the proposal is a self-assessment of the potential contribution to strategy, the financial implications, and the risks. To help the strategy team prioritize initiatives, create a selection matrix with the following criteria.

1. Strategy Impact: To what extent will the project accomplish the goals and objectives? Some, most, all.

2. Stakeholders: What is the impact on the stakeholders, including investors, customers, workforce, suppliers and partners, community and the environment? Response options should range from very negative to very positive for each applicable group.

3. Cost: What is the investment required (operating and capital)? Actual estimate.

4. Cost Savings: What cost savings are expected as a result of this project? Actual estimate.

5. Revenue Change: What changes in revenue are expected as a result of this project? Actual estimate.

6. Risk Severity: How severe are the risks associated with the project? Low, medium, high.

7. Risk Probability: What is the likelihood of risk occurrence? Low, medium, high.

Prioritize

Incorporate a rating system for each criterion and organize the results in a table that allows for the comparison of the initiatives by each criterion and the overall score. While leaders are tempted to turn this exercise into a mere mathematical process, the math is not usually accurate or comprehensive enough to make the decision for you. The value of the matrix is in how it helps facilitate the strategy team dialogue and decisions. Once you have a focused strategy, the next question is how do you enable, empower, and engage your talented workforce to deploy the strategy.

Executive Sponsor

The fourth key component of a strategy are the leaders who will be responsible for each goal and initiative. Unless there is executive sponsorship, the initiative will not be a priority for anyone else in the organization. While many great projects are planned and executed at all levels of the organization often without much visibility to the senior executive team, strategic initiatives must be sponsored by a senior executive that has sufficient resources and influence to help overcome the barriers to successful completion. It is tempting to have more than one senior executive working together as the sponsors. While this might work in a perfect world, in most instances when two people are responsible, no one is responsible. I suggest that one senior executive be the main sponsor for a goal or initiative.

ALIGN AND INTEGRATE

The strategy is the link between the stakeholders + compelling directive, AND the people, processes, and measurement. Strategy at its core is a learning process that makes use of organization performance reviews and organization assessments.

Stakeholder Value - Strategies are developed to address the unique needs, wants, and desires of the individual segments. While each segment might not have an individual strategy, the strategies that are developed address the differing needs of the distinct segments. Even when the product or service doesn't change, the marketing media and messages are often adjusted to communicate with the individual segments.

Compelling Directive - Mission and vision inform the strategy which translates the compelling directive into specific goals and objectives. The strategy addresses both aspects of the compelling directive — the mission of today AND the vision of tomorrow.

Enable, Empower, Engage - Strategic goals and objectives inform the plans and programs to develop and leverage the workforce toward accomplishing the overall strategy, mission, and vision.

[Re]Design Systems - Goals and objectives drive the scope and requirements of the [re]design initiative, which is essentially a strategy deployment process. The benefits and results that are produced by the new designs should contribute to the overall strategy. Progress toward the [re]design initiatives should equal progress toward the strategy.

Comprehensive Scorecard - The comprehensive scorecard includes measures of the outcomes and performance levels described in the strategy. The scorecard also includes measures of progress toward the strategy such as [re]design project cost, quality, schedule, and scope (see Chapter 7 for full description).

Organization Performance Review - The strategy is one of three critical dimensions of measurement and review. The dialogue on strategy includes both the improvements that the strategic initiatives have produced AND the progress and performance of individual projects (e.g., cost, quality, schedule, and cost).

Reinforce Behavior - The behaviors and action that support the strategic goals and objectives are reinforced. At the same time, behaviors and actions that do not support the strategic objectives are discouraged.

Learn and Improve - Reflection and learning about the organization informs the strategy development process. Previous strategies are validated, and lessons learned are used to develop refined or new strategies.

LEADER AS ORGANIZATION ARCHITECT

Leaders often have more "great" ideas of what they would like to do than they have resources to do them. The journey to sustainable excellence is not easy nor is it quick. If there were a few quick and easy things you could do to achieve and sustain excellence, someone would have packaged and patented that solution by now.

The journey requires steady progress and persistence on a few key initiatives at a time. In other words, leaders have to focus on the key objectives until they are complete. Leaders have to set the example and prioritize current activities, and sometimes they have to say "no" to really good ideas. At least "no" for now. If it is a great idea, then it can be scheduled for a later time. Painful as it is to wait on a great idea, it's important to remember that when you try to do everything, you end up doing nothing.

Effective leaders of transformation set high but realistic goals that allow people to achieve high quality and avoid ethical dilemmas. One way to ensure that goals are realistic but challenging is to include stakeholders in a collaborative strategy development process. Leaders also must communicate the goals and clear expectations to multiple stakeholders. While communication is essential to deployment, communication by itself is not deployment. Follow up, personal involvement, progress review and reinforcement are needed to ensure the strategy is fully implemented.

Since we have limited resources, goals need to focus on the key leverage points in the system to create the desired results. A strategy is just a starting point. As German military strategist Helmuth von Moltke noted, "No battle plan . . . survives contact with the enemy." Leaders have to regularly review and reflect on the plan and refine it as needed to address what is learned during the process.

REFLECTION QUESTIONS

1. Take a few moments to assess your current strategy.

    Are your current goals clear, specific, and measurable?

    Do your current goals work together as a coherent strategy?

    Does your strategy address the needs of all your key stakeholders?

    Does your strategy include both long- and short-term goals?

Is your strategy realistic and feasible?

Does your strategy stretch you and the organization?

2. Now think about how you and your colleagues develop strategy.

How do you ensure that you have the right data, in the right format, for analysis?

How do you analyze the various external and internal inputs to strategy?

How do you identify goals?

How do you prioritize and choose which group of goals to pursue in the near-term?

How do you ensure your goals are realistic and at the same time stretch the organization?

Strategy is never static. The strategy and specific initiatives continually evolve through implementation. Gone are the days when you could meet once a year, develop a plan, and spend the rest of the year executing the plan. That never really worked for most organizations anyway.

Today, strategy is often an ongoing conversation that emerges as the year unfolds. Yes, you begin with a portfolio of projects but along the way new projects are added, existing projects are refined and adjusted, and some are abandoned. This ambiguity can cause anxiety for some members of your team, but it does help keep the plan relevant to a fast changing dynamic word. The context of the industry will drive the amount of change and frequency of conversations.

The output or strategy is an untested hypothesis. The next

two chapters describe the development and engagement of the workforce and the [re]design processes necessary to put the strategy in place and test it.

5

ENABLE, EMPOWER, ENGAGE

INTRODUCTION

It is a truism to say, "People are our most valuable asset" — but it is also inaccurate.

First, people are not "assets" owned by the company, and talented people won't work for leaders who treat them as chattel. Organization members (employees, volunteers, etc.) are sovereign human beings and stakeholders. As Drucker (2006) points out, we as leaders often need them more than they need us. Second, all too often leader decisions, policies, and behaviors tell a very different story. Instead of valuable assets, leader actions often paint employees as an expense to be minimized and leveraged for maximum profit. This is the equivalent of killing the goose that laid the golden egg.

People are the bridge between strategy development and strategy deployment. While we often present the strategy process activities in a sequence, in reality, the assessment of the workforce capability and capacity is also an input into the development of the strategy. Leaders of high-performing organizations view workforce members as whole people rather than cogs in a machine.

Whole Person

Leaders often value employees for what they can do for them, but do they truly value them as individuals and empathize with what it is like to be them? High-performing organizations are designed to support employees as whole people, not just tools to be used. Such a humanistic viewpoint is not only right, but logical.

If you take a systems view of the organization, you will find that highly qualified, passionate, engaged workers create great customer experiences, which translates to success across the board. This is not a new idea, and it is supported by research and empirical evidence (e.g., Heskett, et al., 1994). The only explanation I can think of for leaders who don't seem to get it is they lack an understanding of the system, have a short-term perspective, or, worse, do not care. Whatever the explanation, not valuing workers as people is a recipe for poor organization performance. Understanding and caring for the whole person helps you attract the best talent.

Four Components

Figure 5-1 Enable, Empower, Engage - System

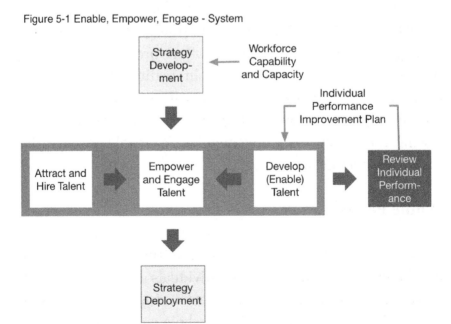

High-performing organizations develop and engage their workforce to accomplish the strategy. Creating a highly qualified and engaged workforce consists of (a) attracting, acquiring and placing talent; (b) developing (enabling) their talent, (c) empowering and engaging talented people, and (d) building a support system for the workforce to facilitate their work and life (Figure 5-1).

ATTRACT

The first step is to assess the current workforce capabilities based on the needs described in the strategy. Then, develop a plan to attract, acquire and place talent to accomplish the strategy. Even when the economy is struggling and many people are looking for work, there is still a shortage of the most talented people. The war for the best talent persists during good times and bad. For some professions, the competition for talent has resulted in assessments and rankings by third party organizations.

One example is the Magnet Recognition Program for hospitals that assesses the quality of nursing and the involvement of nurses in the delivery and improvement of care. Creating an organization that provides and supports meaningful work will attract and retain the best talent. As one high-performing CEO proposed, "if you get very good at finding the right people, everything else will take care of itself."

ENABLE (DEVELOPMENT)

Developing the workforce is a strategic leadership responsibility. A strategy without a capable workforce is a fantasy. Few employees are fully developed with all the knowledge, skills, and abilities (KSAs) that are needed to accomplish the strategy.

So the next step is to assess their current KSAs to develop improvement plans to meet the needs of the strategy.

Building on the concept of the whole person, the improvement plans should be a combination of the needs of the organization and the desires of the individual. The developmental needs are not always directly connected to a specific task in the organization. It is reported that when asked how to become a better manager, Peter Drucker once responded, "Learn how to play the violin." What Drucker meant by that is open for interpretation and discussion. However, for me it is an indication that leading complex organizations, like music, is part art and part science. Don't forget the importance of creativity and art.

Research shows there is a clear link between workforce development and firm performance — including profit. All too often we demand a quantifiable return on our training investment. There are even models that help us evaluate the effectiveness of training and development and the impact on organization performance. These are helpful inputs into the planning and budgeting process. However, there are some training and development activities where the output might not be quite so easy to connect to organization performance. This is where leadership judgement is required.

One of my favorite quotes is the response to the question, "What if you spend all that money on training people, and they leave? What if we don't train them, and they stay?" As Richard Branson advised, "Train people well enough so they can leave, treat them well enough, so they don't want to." Also, it is a waste of time and dangerous to empower and engage people who are not qualified. Empowerment without development is a cruel joke and a recipe for failure.

EMPOWER + ENGAGE

Only qualified employees can be empowered and engaged to make the strategy a reality. This is not surprising given that research shows there is a clear connection between the selection, development, and engagement of employees and firm performance, including the bottom line. (Hatch and Dyer 2004; Harter, Schmidt, and Hayes 2002).

For our purposes, "Empowerment is a combination of motivation to act, authority to do the job, and the enablement to get it done" (Latham, 1995, p. 66). It might seem illogical, but many organizations develop great people and then put them into an organization straightjacket that inhibits their creativity and performance. Leaders can't succeed by micromanaging, yet that is exactly what they all too often attempt to do.

If you have to micromanage employees, you have either hired the wrong people, failed to train them, or both. What is needed are leaders who create an environment that supports the employees reaching their full potential so that they can deliver great products, services, and experiences to the customer or someone who is serving the customer. Once developed, employees can be empowered and engaged to make the compelling directive and strategy a reality. In the next chapter, we focus on creating the organization systems that will create an environment that allows individuals to reach their full potential and make the greatest contribution to the organization possible. This is an environment of innovation and excellence.

SUPPORT

The workforce support system and work environment enable the attraction, development, and engagement of a high performance workforce. While a full description and discussion of the many programs and processes needed to support the workforce is beyond the scope of this book, some aspects of the workforce support system are discussed in Chapter 6. The point: it is important to note that the work environment is influenced by the design of both systems and culture, which influence the degree that people are empowered and encouraged to innovate.

These four components are continually evolving and improving based on input from subsequent strategy updates that influence the overall design of the components and individual performance reviews that influence the refinement of the individual development plans.

ALIGN AND INTEGRATE

While we discuss some distinct people issues in this chapter, people are embedded in all aspects of the organization, so it is no surprise that they are integrated in all eight other leadership activities.

Stakeholder Value - The various workforce segments and their needs inform the design and development of the plans, systems, and practices to enable, empower, and engage the workforce to accomplish the strategy.

Compelling Directive - The mission and vision provide timeless and inspirational guidance to help enable and empower the workforce. The compelling directive provides clear decision-making criteria for those instances when the situation is not covered in the policy manual. The directive also helps to engage people in achieving a purpose larger than themselves.

Focused Strategy – Strategic goals and objectives inform the plans and programs to develop and leverage the workforce toward accomplishing the overall strategy, mission, and vision. Therefore, the capability and capacity of the workforce informs strategy development.

[Re]Design Systems – The workforce is both an input to the [re]design efforts as well as a beneficiary. Enabling, empowering, and engaging the workforce in [re]design efforts is critical to designs that serve the needs of the stakeholders AND the technical requirements. Well-designed systems also benefit the workforce, who have to execute many of those systems.

Comprehensive Scorecard - The comprehensive scorecard includes a group of indicators that measure multiple dimensions of the workforce, including their capability, capacity, level of engagement, etc. The indicators provide information on the success of enable, empower, and engage efforts AND inform improvements to those programs and practices.

Organization Performance Review - Results related to the workforce are part of the organization performance review. But the most important aspect is that the learning that takes place during the reviews helps enable, empower, and engage the leadership team and those they lead. Leaders should emerge better-equipped to provide clear expectations and direction.

Reinforce Behavior - Behaviors that support enabling, empowering, and engaging the workforce are recognized and rewarded. Behaviors that discourage or detract from these activities are not tolerated and never inadvertently rewarded.

Learn and Improve - Learning and improvement is an integral part of enabling and empowering people to contribute toward the overall strategy and compelling directive. Engaging people in learning activities not only improves their capability but also encourages involvement in activities that contribute to the mission and vision.

LEADER AS ORGANIZATION ARCHITECT

While many leaders claim they want a capable and innovative workforce, their behavior often undermines their efforts. Leaders' respect for individuals encourages or discourages empowerment and engagement. Involving and engaging people in the collaborative planning, execution, and improvement of all work will help improve the quality of the solutions. Employee buy-in will also increase with successful implementation.

Organization architect (OA) leaders regularly engage in frank two-way communication with employees. As role models, leaders constantly reinforce employee empowerment and engagement through their behaviors, communications and actions. Leaders understand the connections between employee capability and engagement and enterprise performance and use those insights to develop better organization systems. Also, OA leaders regularly make the rounds with employees to check on key aspects related to employee engagement. Finally, leaders model personal learning and continuous development.

REFLECTION QUESTIONS

1. First, take a few moments to reflect on your own workforce.

    Do you have the best talent available in your industry? Why? Why not?

    Is your workforce highly trained and capable? Why? Why not?

    Is your workforce engaged and using their discretionary energy to accomplish the mission and help make progress toward the vision? Why? Why not?

2. Now think about your systems and processes to attract, develop, and engage the workforce.

    How does your organization systematically attract and hire the best talent available?

    How does your organization systematically develop the workforce to accomplish the strategy?

    How does your organization systematically empower and engage the workforce?

Unfortunately, when faced with short-sighted decisions regarding employees, all too often one hears the excuse, "Well, it is a business." Yes, and all too often a BAD business. When leaders use the excuse that it is a "business" to justify short-term decisions that end up reducing longer-term performance and profitability, they are once again demonstrating a lack of understanding of the organization system and a short-term focus. Or, it could be that they know it is the wrong decision, but they lack the courage to advocate for or do what is best for long-term performance. We need leaders who can produce short-term results without sacrificing longer-term performance.

Leaders who can [re]design the organization systems to create value for all the stakeholders.

6

[RE]DESIGN SYSTEMS

INTRODUCTION

"All improvement takes place project by project . . .
and in no other way."
—Joseph Juran

Unfortunately, many strategy deployment efforts do not achieve the desired change and performance improvement. Why is strategy deployment so hard? One reason might be that it is just more fun to develop plans at a leadership retreat than it is to do the hard work of actually implementing the plans and running an organization.

To address this issue, one successful leader of transformation made the allocation of time between strategy development and deployment explicit: "So we are going to spend 20% of the time on strategy and 80% of the time on deployment, and if we say we are going to do something we are going to do it. We are going to do it [at] world class speed, and we are going to get it done, and we are going to get the results."

Another reason for difficulty is people involved are from various organizational "silos." Each with their own perspective, agenda, and motives. A structured approach to planning and leading change initiatives, along with the discipline to follow through with project details can help address some of these issues.

ORGANIZATION SYSTEM

Strategy deployment and organization transformation are

inextricably linked. Organization design and transformation are driven by the overall strategy, goals, objectives, and priorities. In other words, "form follows function," thus organization strategy guides the design changes to the organization, systems, and processes. Organization systems are not simply the digital computer systems, although those are part of the organization system. Organization systems consist of the flow of activity, resources, information, and energy throughout the organization. The need for systems in organizations is not a new idea: Chinese philosopher Mo-Tze identified the need over 2500 years ago:

> *"Whoever pursues a business in this world must have a system. A business which has attained success without a system does not exist. From ministers and generals down to the hundreds of craftsmen, every one of them has a system. The craftsmen employ the ruler to make a square and the compass to make a circle. All of them, both skilled and unskilled, use this system. The skilled may at times accomplish a circle and a square by their own dexterity. But with a system, even the unskilled may achieve the same result, though dexterity they have none. Hence, every craftsman possesses a system as a model. Now, if we govern the empire, or a large state, without a system as a model, are we not even less intelligent than a common craftsman?"*
> — Mo-Tze (a.k.a. Miscius), 500 BCE (Wu, 1928, p. 226).

Systems Framework

The organization system includes many systems, sub-systems, and processes. It is helpful to categorize these systems into a few manageable categories (Figure 6-1). These systems are grouped into three levels of systems: value creation, enablers, and guidance.

Figure 6-1 Organization System

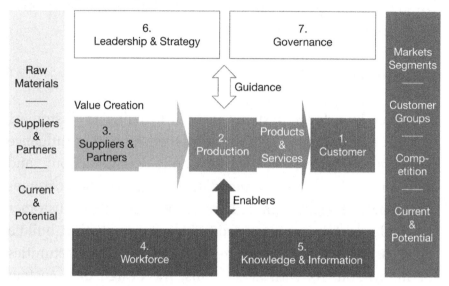

Value creation systems include the entire value chain from understanding customer requirements and designing and developing products to the supplier management, operations, and delivery and customer relationships systems. Depending on the nature of the products, these systems are often combinations of physical, knowledge, and creative processes, often with the need for bespoke (custom) execution.

Enabler systems support the continuous improvement of all systems including value creation systems as well as the guidance systems. Enabler systems include people support processes to help humans learn, develop, and innovate. Also, these systems provide performance measures and a review processes that produce new insights and knowledge.

Guidance systems provide direction and resources to the value creation and support systems as well as the enabler systems. Guidance systems include leadership; strategy development and deployment; governance; ethical, legal, and regulatory; and social and environmental sustainability. These are knowledge and creative systems that facilitate innovative solutions and information flows.

1. Customer

Customer knowledge systems include listening to customers (current and potential); determining the factors that influence purchase decisions, satisfaction and dissatisfaction; and analyzing and using customer data to improve the customer experience. Insights gained from an effective customer knowledge system are also used to improve marketing, build a more customer-focused culture, and identifying opportunities for innovation. As with all systems, the design of a custom customer knowledge system is based on the unique needs of the organization and the strategy system.

The customer experience systems involve the organization's processes for identifying and innovating product offerings that create memorable customer experiences. Experience systems also include mechanisms for supporting customer use of those products and for building a customer culture within your workforce. The aim of these efforts is to build relationships with customers and increase their engagement with the organization. Custom customer experience systems are designed from the perspective of the customer and they address all aspects that directly influence the customer experience. Key considerations and issues for customer system design include (selected):

Voice of the Customer - Developing a comprehensive view of customers, including both hard and soft measures. Listening posts for current and potential customers and listening to complaints.

Determining Satisfaction - Measuring satisfaction and dissatisfaction, including comparisons.

Analysis and Use of Customer Knowledge - Customer and market segmentation, customer requirements, and using customer data for improvement.

Product and Service Offering - Design for the desired customer experience.

Support and Access Mechanisms - Design for the desired customer experience, including complaint resolution system.

2. Production

The production system includes the key value creation and support processes that produce the products and services. The operations system transforms the inputs from supplier and partners to create ever-increasing value for customers. Operations are designed for both execution and continuous learning and improvement to meet the unique needs of the organization and their operating environment. Key design considerations for the production system include (selected):

Customer and Stakeholder Focus - Translating customer and stakeholder needs into process requirements.

Design - Leveraging organizational knowledge and new technology to develop innovative designs to meet and exceed customer and stakeholder requirements.

Management - Managing the day-to-day operations to ensure the processes meet and exceed the customer and stakeholder requirements.

Assessment - Measuring and evaluating work process performance from multiple perspectives (effectiveness, efficiency, etc.).

Imrovement - Continuous process improvement to achieve better performance and improve products and services.

3. Suppliers and Partners

One reason the supplier and partnership systems are separate and distinct is they deal with the integration of external suppliers and partners. The supplier and partnership systems address how the organization designs, manages, and improves the way they involve suppliers, partners, contractors, and collaborators to accomplish the work that delivers customer value and achieves overall organizational success and sustainability. The focus of the partnership systems is on designing and deploying a custom work system to meet the unique needs of the organization and the operating environment. Design considerations and issues (selected):

Selection - Supplier and partner selection and management to enhance the customer experience. Better inputs = better outputs.

Systems Thinking - Understanding the organization as an integrated system of processes and people (workforce, suppliers, partners, collaborators, etc.).

Work Placement - Developing work placement strategies that leverage the organization's core competencies.

Management - Coordinating the mix of workforce, suppliers and partners, contractors and collaborators to deliver the products and services, as well as execute the value-creation and support processes.

Controlling Costs - Preventing defects, service errors, and rework to minimize costs.

4. Workforce

Workforce systems address the many aspects of attracting, developing, engaging, and supporting the workforce. Attract and acquire systems focus on the overall capability (knowledge, skills, abilities) of the workforce as well as the capacity. These systems are designed to ensure a workforce that is capable and has the capacity needed to ensure sustainable high performance that is aligned and integrated with the organization's strategic goals, objectives, and action plans.

The workforce development system ensures the continuous development of leaders and the workforce to support the organization's core competencies and strategy. The empowerment and engagement system focuses on supporting high performance work and innovation that is aligned and integrated with the organization's strategic goals, objectives, and action plans.

Finally, the support system focuses on key workforce health, safety and security including policies, services, benefits to create and maintain a high-performance work environment that encourages workforce engagement. Support systems ensure the well-being of the workforce as well as encourages engagement that is aligned and integrated with the organization's strategy The systems work together to provide a highly talented and engaged workforce that is continuously learning and innovating. Key design issues and considerations include (selected):

Needs Assessment - Evaluating the workforce capability and capacity (knowledge, skills and abilities) needs of the organization. Identifying gaps in workforce capability and capacity.

Segmentation - Identifying key workforce groups and segments to develop engagement strategies for the unique needs of the different groups.

Acquire and Retain Talent - Recruiting, hiring, placing, and retaining a high performance workforce.

Career Progression - Mapping career paths for the various workforce and leader segments.

Succession Planning - Creating a pipeline of highly qualified replacements, including leaders.

Services - Identifying and developing workforce services that enhance workforce engagement.

Reinforcement - Creating incentives that support a high-performance and engaged workforce.

5. Knowledge and Information

Knowledge and information systems support the measurement of performance, the analysis of the systems, and the capture and dissemination of the knowledge derived from the analysis. The measurement systems focus on the selection and use of data and information for performance measurement to support the operation and improvement of systems throughout the organization. The analysis system addresses the systematic review and analysis of the organization's scorecard results to support the strategic leadership and value production systems.

The Knowledge Management (KM) System addresses how the organization collects, manages and disseminates knowledge throughout the organization. KM systems are designed to ensure the quality and availability of needed data, information, software, and hardware for the organization's stakeholders including the workforce, suppliers, partners, customers, and society. Knowledge management systems include: systems and processes, culture, individuals, and technology. Design considerations and issues (selected):

The Big Picture - An enterprise systems approach to building a comprehensive scorecard.

Measure Selection - Criteria and process for evaluating and selecting potential measures.

Data Collection - Systematic approaches to ensuring credible and reliable data and information.

Comparisons - Understanding how your organization stacks up against industry leaders, world class organizations, and competitors.

Analysis - Assess results (levels, trends and comparisons) on three dimensions of stakeholder value, progress relative to strategy and competitive performance, and system performance including the organization's ability to rapidly respond to changing needs.

Translating Findings into Action - Prioritization of opportunities and deployment of actions to improve performance.

Managing Knowledge - Accuracy, Integrity, Reliability, Timeliness, Security, and Confidentiality and — maybe most important — Easy Access and User Friendly distribution systems.

6. Leadership and Strategy

At the upper echelons in an organization, it is difficult to separate leadership from strategy. Even at lower levels in the organization, leadership is inextricably linked to strategy translation and deployment. The leadership and strategy system is a system of systems. In other words, it is a systematic approach to connecting and guiding the other systems, connecting the systematic processes for Chapters 2 through 10.

Regardless of your level in the organization you need a systematic approach to:

- understand your stakeholders needs;

- develop or translate the mission, vision, and strategy of the organization to your part of the organization;

- enable, empower, and engage your workforce to accomplish the mission, vision, and strategy;

- [re]design systems and processes under your purview to improve performance of the overall system and measure the performance of those systems and processes;

- periodically review performance in order to make changes and reinforce the desired behavior and performance; and

- reflect, learn, and refine the strategy.

While strategy is embedded in the leadership system, a distinct and detailed system to support those elements is often helpful. Strategic management is often a complicated endeavor involving the coordinated efforts of people across the organization. For many organizations, the supporting processes for strategy development and project management systems needed for strategy deployment can be complex and require multiple processes. Strategic management activities and issues include (selected):

Environmental Scan and Analysis - Fact-based understanding of the internal and external environments.

Strategy Creation - Leveraging core competencies to develop externally focused strategies.

Feasibility Assessment - Balance, goal refinement, and prioritization.

Action Plan Development - Identifying the product, service and operational changes needed to accomplish the strategy.

Follow-through - Implementation, tracking, and refinement of action plans.

Sustaining Improvements - Ensuring the changes become the new standard.

7. Governance

Governance systems focus on ensuring accountability, transparency, and protection of stakeholder interests. The governance system is aligned and integrated with the organization's unique context and operating environment. Also included are the legal, ethical, and regulatory systems which are designed to ensure legal and ethical behavior in all organization activities and transactions. Included in these systems is the development of processes and practices to anticipate stakeholder concerns with current and future products, services, and operations. Also, systems are included to address the social and environmental aspects of the organization, products, services, and operations. Systems are designed to align and integrate the stakeholders' interests and the organization's unique mission, context, and external operating environment. Design issues and considerations (selected):

Accountability - Ensuring accountability at the top and throughout the organization.

Transparency - Systematic selection of information, decisions, and policies for sharing inside and outside the organization.

Independent Audits - Ensuring accurate reporting through independent internal and external audits.

Evaluation - Assessing CEO, senior leader, and board member performance.

Impact on Society - Identifying and addressing adverse impacts of products, services, and operations on society.

Proactive - Anticipating public concerns with current and planned products, services, and operations.

Ethical Behavior - Promoting and assuring ethical behavior in all transactions.

When embarking on an organization redesign journey, it is often best to begin with the top-level systems and let those become the guide for the sub-systems. The first place to begin is usually with the Leadership System which is a "system of systems" and connects several of the other top-level systems. Ideally, these systems are aligned and integrated to create a high-performing organization that creates sustainable value for multiple stakeholders.

An enterprise process model is, as one CEO put it, "a logical assembly of processes that you need to do to run your business." While the categorization of organization systems varies slightly among the many excellence models such as the Malcolm Baldrige National Quality Award in the United States, the European Foundation for Quality Management, and a variety of country and company excellence award programs, they all have some version of the seven systems groups presented here.

While these are typical major systems in an organization, this list is not exhaustive. There are many more systems and processes embedded in these systems throughout the organization. How you label and classify your systems will depend on the particular model that you are using to assist in your improvement efforts. The good news is the design process and framework are applicable to your systems regardless of you the classification scheme you choose or create.

Individual System Components

While organization systems come in a wide variety of shapes and sizes, most are composed of seven basic components (Figure 6-2).

Figure 6-2 Basic System Components

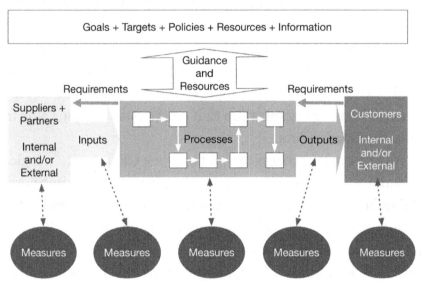

1. Customers (external and internal) and their requirements for the outputs.

2. Outputs (a.k.a. deliverables) are clearly defined, including physical products, services, and information. Specifications for the deliverables are clear and explicit and drive the design of the process. This varies with the nature of the system. See more on this later in this chapter.

3. Processes (activities and interconnections) are explicitly and clearly defined and understood. Internal customer and supplier relationships and requirements are clear and explicit.

4. Inputs (internal and external) are identified and requirements clearly and explicitly defined.

5. Suppliers (internal and external) are identified for each input. Performance and relationship requirements are explicit and clear.

6. Measurements for each of the first five components are identified and operationally defined. Results levels, trends, and comparisons are measured at several places along the value chain or processes.

7. Guidance and resources are identified and allocated (people, capital, technology, etc.) to make the system work. Relevant guidance related to strategy and organization culture is identified. Goals and performance targets are set and periodically compared to actual performance.

The design process addresses all seven components to create integrated systems that are aligned and continuously improving.

[Re]Designing Individual Systems

The [re]design of organization systems requires that the designer or architect combine systems thinking with design thinking in a process that is both creative and inductive, and at the same time, scientific and deductive. Design projects can be organized into a three distinct but related phases including (1) Discovery, (2) Design, and (3) Develop, Deploy, and Iterate (Figure 6-3).

Figure 6-3 Three Phase [Re]Design Project

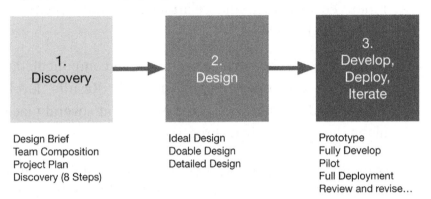

Design Brief   Ideal Design   Prototype
Team Composition   Doable Design   Fully Develop
Project Plan   Detailed Design   Pilot
Discovery (8 Steps)   Full Deployment
                                               Review and revise...

The first two phases of the [re]design process (Discovery and Design) are primarily inductive, creative processes that generate new insights, ideas, and solutions. The third and last phase of the [re]design process (Develop, Deploy, and Iterate) is often a more deductive, iterative testing and development process.

A design project begins with a comprehensive discovery phase. This discovery phase is one of the key differences between a design approach to organization system design and other methods of improving organizational processes and performance. Once the discovery is complete, the new system is [re]designed. At least three versions of the design are developed during this phase, including an ideal design, a doable design, and a detailed design. The last phase is the development, testing, and deployment of the system. The Design Framework provides the flexible structure to guide the [re]design of any system in the organization.

DESIGN FRAMEWORK

The Design Framework provides a flexible yet systematic

approach to designing organizational systems for all types of organizations: commercial, non-profit, and governmental (Figure 6-4). While the framework is presented here in a sequence, in practice the process is a bit messier and often winds around in an iterative exploration of considerations and options. Consequently, the approach to design here is a flexible framework as opposed to a sequential procedure.

Figure 6-4 Design Framework

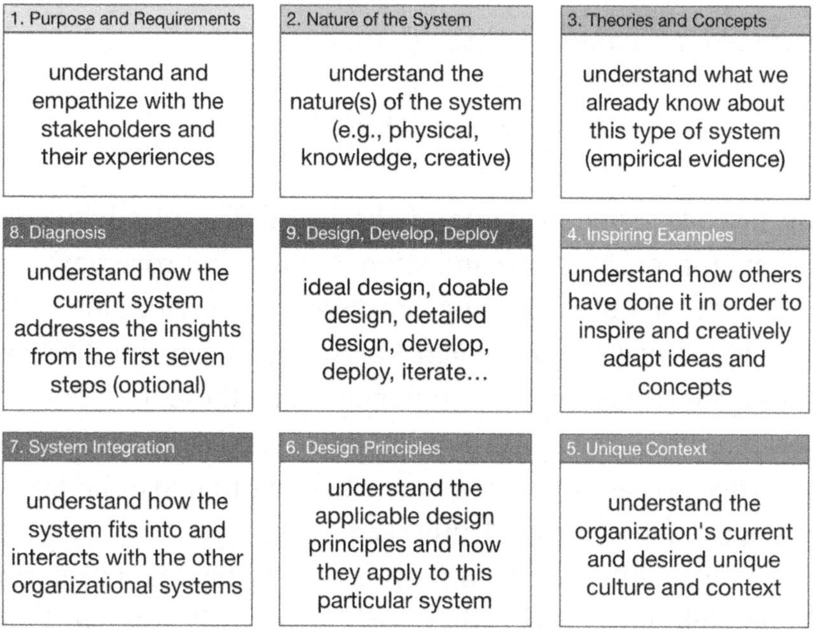

1. Purpose and Requirements	2. Nature of the System	3. Theories and Concepts
understand and empathize with the stakeholders and their experiences	understand the nature(s) of the system (e.g., physical, knowledge, creative)	understand what we already know about this type of system (empirical evidence)
8. Diagnosis	9. Design, Develop, Deploy	4. Inspiring Examples
understand how the current system addresses the insights from the first seven steps (optional)	ideal design, doable design, detailed design, develop, deploy, iterate...	understand how others have done it in order to inspire and creatively adapt ideas and concepts
7. System Integration	6. Design Principles	5. Unique Context
understand how the system fits into and interacts with the other organizational systems	understand the applicable design principles and how they apply to this particular system	understand the organization's current and desired unique culture and context

The first eight steps (outer boxes) of the Design Framework form the discovery phase. The process begins with a clear understanding of the purpose and requirements of the system and ends with a diagnosis of the existing system (as applicable). The discovery then seeks out information on the key design considerations that will help inform the design phase. The design phase consists of three steps: the ideal conceptual design, the doable conceptual design, and finally the detailed design. The final component includes the development, deployment, and continuous improvement of the system. The Design Framework provides a structured but flexible approach to help you navigate the design process. As we explore each component of the Design Framework further, we will include a discussion of a leadership system as our example to help illustrate the components. The leadership system is a system of systems and integrates aspects of several other top-level systems. A leadership system includes systematic methods to address the leadership activities discussed in Chapters 2 through 10.

DISCOVERY

The discovery phase is one of the key differences between a design approach to organization system improvement and other methods of improving processes and performance. The first eight steps of the Design Framework form the discovery phase. These first eight components are the springboard to the creative design and development process. An expanded discovery process is a key enabler helping to make the leap to an aligned and integrated approach.

While we often want to jump to solutions, taking the time to complete a thorough discovery process will set the design team up to leap from where ever you are to an aligned and integrated system. The challenge is to integrate and incorporate all of these elements into the design team's thinking without inhibiting the design team's creativity. While a design approach that includes a discovery phase will help you leap to an aligned and integrated design, that design still requires development, testing, deployment, and continuous improvement. The discovery process begins with a clear purpose and requirements for the system.

1. Purpose and Requirements

Organization design is an indicator of leadership intent, and the purpose is the first step in defining that intent.

Purpose

The first step in organization system design is to define the intent or purpose of the particular system being designed. During this first step, develop a clear understanding of the purpose(s) for the system; identify the stakeholder needs, wants and desires; and identify key features, functions and components of the system and the associated requirements.

You might start by asking the basic question, "Why do we need this organization or management system?" A clear understanding the purpose(s) of the system will provide the design team with a solid foundation and touchstone for future discovery and design decisions. The purposes for an organization or management system can come from a variety of sources and inputs, including leaders, regulations, industry standards and so forth. Typically, the leaders will define the need for the system and its basic purpose.

Management Requirements

With a clear purpose identified, the next step is to identify the requirements that will help fulfill that purpose. What are the main capabilities needed for this system, including the key components and requirements. The key components are often identified by existing models or standards. In addition to the components, what are the key requirements of the system? The result of the first two elements (purpose and management requirements) exercise is the first part of a formal design brief. A design brief is a formal document that captures the key project requirements and parameters. The design brief will evolve throughout the discovery process. Up to this point, the input has been primarily from management, which is a great starting point.

Stakeholder's Needs

The last step in the purpose and requirements component is to understand the key stakeholders and their requirements. First, identify the key stakeholders for this particular system or process. The six stakeholder groups identified in Chapter 2 make a good starting point. The six stakeholder groups are the customers (internal and external), the workforce, the suppliers and partners (external and internal), the investors, the community and the natural environment. However, the six groups are often too large and general to be useful for a specific system design. Consequently, the task here is to get specific. Once the specific stakeholders are identified, use an empathy profile approach to understand their experiences with the system.

Example - Leadership System Purpose and Requirements

An explicit leadership system (LS) has several purposes: aligning and integrating the enterprise management systems, making leadership decisions and actions explicit so they can be communicated, and developing leaders at all levels.

Align and Integrate

A key aspect of leadership is the ability to influence the actions of people and engage leaders and the workforce in purposeful actions that are aligned with and contribute to the improvement of the organization's performance. An explicit leadership system enables the alignment and integration of the various other management activities, practices, and processes into a coherent and congruent approach. As one CEO noted, it provides the glue that holds the larger system together. As another CEO mentioned, "I think that most people don't understand all the pieces... They understand them, but they don't fit them together in an integration and show how they all fit together to work together."

In addition, when performance measurement is integrated in the leadership system, it helps to drive results that include both breakthroughs and incremental improvements. As one participant responded when asked about the purpose of his LS: ". . . number one, I think it drives results." So one purpose of the LS is to integrate and align the organization's strategy, action, and results.

Make Leadership Decisions and Actions Explicit

Another purpose is to make the decisions and actions of leaders explicit so they can be communicated, assessed, and improved. As one CEO said, "You got to stay in touch, you've got to have the employees engaged, and you've got to make sure that the systems tools are being used."

One purpose of the LS is to provide a framework for the purposeful interaction of leaders with people throughout the organization. A formal LS enables leaders to systematically review progress and work with people to adjust their actions to improve performance and progress. Another CEO mentioned, "Deming says if you can't...describe what you're doing as a process, then you don't know what you're doing." Another CEO recalled when the consultant asked him to describe his leadership system: "I began to describe it and she said now draw it for me. I really couldn't draw it." Without an explicit system, it is very difficult to communicate your leadership approach to others, examine your approach, reflect on it, improve it, and teach it to others.

Develop Leaders at All Levels

An explicit LS enables the development of leaders by helping them think about how they integrate their personal leadership style with the leadership activities described in the leadership system. Several CEOs have found that an explicit leadership system "made it easier for people to understand how to lead and what we meant by it." One participant noted that "after we came up with the leadership system we realized we had all the pieces, but we didn't have a way to train people and make this a living leadership system, one that you could point to and say this is how we think and this is how we do things." Developing a pipeline of leaders helps ensure continuity when leaders turn over. This continuity helps to keep your organization from being dependent on any one individual leader.

2. Nature of the System

Systems and processes differ in many ways, but the nature of the system will guide many design decisions. The nature of the system influences design decisions such as the level of process control required and the level of specificity of the various process steps and activities. There are four basic types or natures of systems, including physical processes (manufacturing, transportation, etc.); knowledge or information processes (loan processing, insurance claims, etc.); creative processes (strategy development, product development, etc.); and the degree of customization required (bespoke).

Physical systems can and often do have many technical constraints that must be dealt with during the design process. Also, many physical processes require a high degree of standardization and focus on conformance to reduce variation. Knowledge systems and processes provide the necessary accurate information to the decision makers with the least amount of effort and cost. Creative systems and processes tend to be less effective when the degree of process specificity and standardization are high. Structure can enhance the level of creativity — but only up to a point, and then additional structure beyond that point will impede or reduce creativity.

The challenge in designing creative systems is to have just enough structure and no more. The last type of system is a variation on the previous three types, and it is the degree to which these systems or processes have to produce customized or "bespoke" outputs based on a variety of needs of the customer or user.

These four types of processes are not mutually exclusive. Many systems are composed of combinations of two or sometimes all four types of processes — physical, knowledge, creative, and bespoke.

Physical Systems

The first step is to identify the physical components of the system. Some systems and processes are primarily physical, such as manufacturing, transportation, nuclear power, etc. The design of physical systems is quite different than knowledge or creative processes. Physical systems can and often do have many engineering and scientific knowledge constraints that must be dealt with during the design process.

Also, many physical processes require a high degree of standardization to reduce variation and ensure safety. While designers of automated physical systems have to deal with engineering challenges, they often have fewer human issues to overcome. However, many to most physical systems involve some integration of humans to perform certain tasks or make certain decisions. Integrating humans can provide additional options but at the same time adds constraints or limitations. If the system can be automated, then that will impact the remaining design decisions. Generally speaking, humans make poor machines. Thus, if a system can be automated, it probably should be.

Since controls often impede other desirable characteristics (e.g., creativity and innovation), the objective is to include only as much control as is necessary to meet the requirements and nature of the system. While some systems are primarily physical systems, there are often knowledge and sometimes creative dimensions or components integrated in these systems.

Knowledge Systems

The second step is to identify the knowledge components of the system. Most systems involve information or knowledge of some sort. Sometimes the knowledge in the form of an algorithm and sometimes the knowledge informs human decisions and activities. The first question then is: To what extent does the system require humans to make decisions or take action based on the information? The portions of the system that do not require humans to make decisions are candidates for digital automation.

However, many knowledge systems and processes have to be designed to enable and engage human minds as a key component in the system. The goal in these situations is to provide the necessary, accurate information to the decision makers with the least amount of effort and cost. A loan process, for example, includes components of information transfer that do not require a human decision. Other components do require human intervention, such as the decisions to loan, set an interest rate, etc. Some knowledge systems and processes serve more creative purposes.

Creative Systems

Some knowledge processes are administrative or analytical in nature, and some require creativity. The third step is to identify the creative components of the system. In this step the task is to determine the degree to which the system allows and encourages creativity and innovation. This is often at odds with the degree to which control is needed in the system. Creative systems and processes tend to be less effective when the degree of process specificity and standardization are high. Structure can enhance the level of creativity but only up to a point and then additional structure beyond that point will impede or reduce creativity. The challenge in designing creative systems is to have just enough structure and no more.

Many management systems such as leadership systems and strategic management systems require a high degree of creativity. So the trick is to figure out just how much structure is needed to enhance the creative processes and no more. This type of system is often over-engineered in management's never-ending attempt to predict performance. However, when it is over-engineered, they get predictably poor performance. If you want creativity and innovation, you will have to learn to live with some ambiguity.

Bespoke?

The fourth step is to determine the degree to which flexibility is needed during execution of the system to provide custom products and services to the customer or user. How flexible does this system or process need to be to effectively address variation in users, situations, purposes, etc.? A high level of customization is needed for processes that need to be adjusted to meet the needs of different users (training and education, food service, etc.). Does this system or process need to be designed so it can be used by a wide variety of cultures, teams, individuals? Physical processes tend to require less flexibility and are typically more standardized than knowledge of creative processes.

However, there are instances where the physical processes require flexibility in execution. Service industries often deal with physical components (food, hotel properties, etc.) that have to be either modified or combined in various ways to serve the various needs of a variety of customers. The trick is to determine early in the design process the need for customization in the process so that the right degree of flexibility can be designed into the system.

Example – Nature of a Leadership System

A leadership system is a combination of knowledge and creative components that requires a high level of customization depending on the particular leader and follower combination. Some have proposed that you can't systematize leadership.

However, knowledge and creative systems often do not require formal steps in a rigid sequence.

A LS is by its nature a combination of knowledge processes, leadership practices, and cultural values and norms. Consequently, the design of an effective LS is characterized by flexible frameworks, principles, information and activities that enhance the art of leadership. Once one understands the purpose, requirements and nature of the system, the next question is: What do we already know about this type of system?

3. Theories and Concepts

Kurt Lewin proposed, "There is nothing as practical than a good theory." I know what many of you are thinking: "Are you kidding me? Management theory, really?" The good news is there is no heavy-handed management theory required for this process. However, an understanding of the empirical evidence regarding what works, what we know doesn't work, and under what conditions, is useful for any management design endeavor.

Jeffrey Pfeffer and Robert Sutton, in their book *Hard Facts, Dangerous Half-Truths and Total Nonsense: Profiting from Evidence-Based Management,* make the point that practitioners' actions and practices are often not based on the latest scientific theory. In fact, their practices have already been demonstrated not to work. This is the risk of ignoring management theory: you might end up endlessly reinventing a broken wheel.

> *"It is not clear how we got to this point. It is hard for one to imagine an architect not taking into consideration important scientific evidence (e.g., metallurgy) when designing a new building"* (Latham, 2012, pp. 12-13).

Questions to ask:

Who are the leading thinkers in this area or system (e.g., strategic management).

What are the established theories related to this particular area or system?

What do they tell us about the design of the system?

Depending on the particular system, this can be a large task. It is usually impractical for the design team to study all the relevant literature on a particular process or system. That's where subject matter experts come in.

Subject Matter Experts

Unfortunately, we seldom have the time to do all the research that would be required to do this step well. Consequently, subject matter experts (SMEs) are often included on the design team to provide this knowledge as needed throughout the design process. Also, there is the complexity of context and the cross-disciplinary nature of most organization systems (e.g., psychology, sociology, business, and systems theory). One way to avoid the team getting bogged down doing research on the key theories and concepts is to include applicable SMEs on the design team. Ideally, these SMEs also have an understanding and appreciation for the other disciplines in the system. In other words people with depth in a particular area, but also breadth in a variety of areas enabling them to work on cross-disciplinary projects such as organization design teams.

Example - Leadership System Theories

The leadership system that is described in this book is a result of both practice and a CEO study that was published in

2013 (Latham, 2013a, 2013b). The nine components printed in Chapters 2 through 10 form the basic framework for the leadership system model (Figure 6-5).

According to our research, there were four key leadership theories that were most likely to inform sustainable excellence, including transformation, transactional, servant, and spiritual leadership. For more on the specific links between these theories and the leadership system see Latham (2013a and 2013b).

Figure 6-5 Leadership System Components

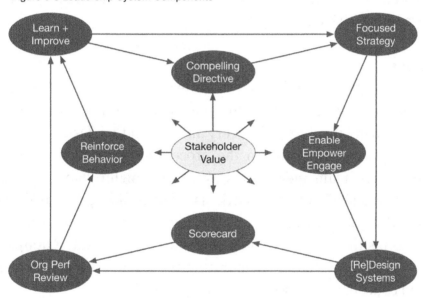

4. Inspiring Examples

World-class examples help to bring theories and concepts alive. This review of example designs can help clarify the concepts and application, thus inspiring the design team's creative thinking.

There has been a lot of emphasis and effort put into benchmarking over the years. When done right, studying and creatively adapting key characteristics from example designs as part of a design thinking process can help you leapfrog the competition. Some have noted that benchmarking dooms you to following the leaders. Experience suggests that in some circumstances, examples can be a double-edged sword. While it can help to clarify and inspire a custom design for your particular situation, it can also short-circuit the creative process. Design teams will occasionally stop working on a custom design once they see an example that they think will fit the organization. While this saves time, in the end it is not as effective as a true custom design that is inspired or informed by the examples. So proceed with caution.

Uses

Examples are used at two different points in the design process. First, high-level conceptual design examples are used here during the initial discovery and conceptual design phases. Examples at this point in the process are particularly useful for design team members who are not highly knowledge of or experienced with the particular system being designed. As one CEO noted, examples can be very helpful to "bring alive" concepts that are in the early stages of development. Examples can also be useful for invigorating the often abstract theories and concepts discussed in the previous step.

Second, detailed examples are used during the detailed design phase to provide tangible options and ideas. At this point, specific examples are useful for the design of the individual components of the system or process. Remember, some of the greatest insights and creative inspirations come from examples outside of your particular industry. In the words of one of my favorite architects, Norman Foster: "Everything Inspires Me, Sometimes I Think I See Things Others Don't."

Example - Leadership System Inspiring Examples

In the beginning, which seems to date back to 1997 and Boeing Airlift and Tanker's efforts to develop a leadership system, a few of the early adopters had to start from scratch without the benefit of examples to follow (e.g., Spong and Collard, 2009). These trailblazers developed leadership systems that were conceptual diagrams of the key activities and their relationships using only their experience, ingenuity, the requirements from the Baldrige criteria and advice from consultants.

Once these early examples were published and presented at annual Quest for Excellence Conferences (e.g., Clarke 2002), other organizations were able to leverage these examples and creatively adapt the concepts to their own organizations. One CEO noted that he ". . . then read every Baldrige application I could get because those intrigued me, because I really got into these categories and specifically leadership, customer market focus, and process management – it really, really intrigued me a lot." Leadership System examples are available from a variety of sources including, Award Application Summaries for the MBNQA recipients since 1999 that are available free for download from the NIST website. See Resources at: http://organizationdesignstudio.com/recreate-resources/

5. Unique Context

One of the main reasons to go through the trouble of developing a custom design is so the design fits the unique characteristics of the organization and situation. For example, the appropriate production system for the local retail outlet is likely to be a bit different from the appropriate system for a multi-national manufacturing company with operations around the world.

To design a system to fit the unique characteristics of the

organization, first identify the key organizational factors that impact the design of the particular system. Organization factors can vary widely but are generally organized into a few categories including the external environment, strategy, value chain (including industry, geography, and technology), the workforce (types of employees), and the culture (values, symbols, rituals, and heroes). While many systems are impacted by only a few contextual factors, leadership and strategy development and deployment systems are influenced by many to most of the contextual factors. Understanding the unique context of the organization is an important step in designing a custom leadership system that fits the particular organization.

Example - Leadership System Context Considerations

While leadership systems often include similar components across a variety of organizations and industries, the details of these components vary depending on several context factors.

Workforce profile - The types of work and qualifications of the workforce will influence the appropriate leadership approach including empowerment, communication, etc.

Culture - Current and desired culture (mission, vision, values), stakeholder segments, and needs all influence key components of the leadership system.

Organization size and geography - Are leaders and followers in the same physical location or are they virtual? What country cultures are included?

The context of the organization not only indicates what is relevant and important to the particular organization, but it also helps inform the identification of key characteristics in the design of the leadership system. These characteristics are often called design principles.

6. Design Principles

Design principles are the desired characteristics of the new system. They are cross-cutting and are used to inform the design. There are eight established design principles that have proven useful for developing high-performing organization and management systems. The design team must understand the established eight design principles and how they apply to the system being designed. The design team begins with established management system design principles such as balance, sustainability convenience (user-friendly), alignment, learning, etc., and then they identify any additional characteristics or design principles to consider during the diagnosis and design phases.

Balance

The principle of balance is the degree to which the system creates value for multiple stakeholders. While the ideal is to develop a design that maximizes the value for all the key stakeholders, the designer often has to compromise and balance the needs of the various stakeholders.

Example - The leadership system has to balance the needs of the stakeholders throughout the activities including the key cornerstones of stakeholders, strategy, systems, and the scorecard. The concept of balance is integrated into decision-making throughout the leadership system.

Congruence

The principle of congruence is the degree to which the system components are aligned and consistent with each other and the other organizational systems, strategies, scorecard, stakeholders, culture, and context.

Example - The nine key components of the leadership system are all related. Near the end of Chapters 2 through 10, there is a section that details the alignment and integration considerations for all nine leadership system components.

Convenience

The principle of convenience is the degree to which the system is designed to be as convenient as possible for the participants to implement (a.k.a. user-friendly). The system includes specific processes, procedures and controls only when necessary.

Example - While it is easy to make the leadership system complex, if you want people to actually use it, you will want to keep the fundamentals as simple as possible. The good news is the details of systems are documented and do not need to be remembered if leaders embed the leadership system in the culture from top to bottom.

Coordination

The principle of coordination is the degree to which the system components are integrated and work in harmony with the other (internal and external) systems, processes, components, and stakeholders toward common objectives. This is beyond congruence and is achieved when the individual components of a system operate as a fully interconnected unit.

Example - The alignment and integration notes at the end of Chapters 2 through 10 cover both alignment (congruence) and integration.

Elegance

The principle of elegance is the degree of system complexity vs. benefit. The system includes only enough complexity as is necessary to meet the stakeholder's needs. In other words, keep the design as simple as possible while delivering the desired benefits. This often requires looking at the system in new ways. The trick is to design organizations with just enough of the right structure and incentives and no more.

Managers want to manage. Otherwise, they feel like they are not doing their job. Maybe it is time to get rid of management as traditionally practiced and make managers designers of systems that have the right structure, features, and functions to facilitate stakeholder engagement and performance.

Example - The leadership system is a system of systems and thus difficult to simplify at the strategic level. However, the fundamentals of each activity can be designed to be only as complex as required by the context. In the case of the leadership system, leadership at the top of the organization is complex but you can take the same basic leadership system structure and apply it in much less complex ways at lower levels in the organization.

Human

The human principle is the degree to which the participants in the system are able to find joy, purpose, and meaning in their work. Work is personal, and that's a good thing (or it should be).

Example – The design of the leadership system must be sufficiently flexible to allow for individual leaders to make it their own. While all work is personal, leadership is particularly personal for both the leader and the follower. The leadership system needs to allow for this flexibility so the leader can use it effectively with a wide variety of people and situations.

Learning

The principle of learning is the degree to which opportunities for reflection and learning (learning loops) are designed into the system. Reflection and learning are built into the system at key points to encourage single- and double-loop learning from experience to improve future implementation and to systematically evaluate the design of the system itself.

Example – The leadership system has learning built into several key components, and it is specifically built into the organization performance review process and the learning and improvement processes.

Sustainability

The sustainability principle is the degree to which the system effectively meets the near- and long-term needs of the current stakeholders without compromising the ability of future generations of stakeholders to meet their own needs. Dimensions include the economic, environmental and societal needs related to the system (adapted from UN 1987).

Example - The leadership system integrates stakeholder value for all six stakeholder groups into all the leadership activities.

7. System Integration

> *"Always design a thing by considering it in its next larger context — a chair in a room, a room in a house, a house in an environment, an environment in a city plan."* — Eliel Saarinen.

Most (if not all) organization and management systems are part of a larger group of systems that eventually combine to manage the overall enterprise. A system perspective of the larger enterprise management system helps design systems that are congruent, aligned, and integrated. In addition, the systems perspective allows organizations to look beyond the immediate goal or desired outcome of a particular system and identify key leverage points in the overall system to achieve their objectives and purposes. Systems align with the other organization design cornerstones (stakeholders, strategy, and scorecard), culture (value, heroes, symbols, and rituals), and the context of the organization (industry, geography, and technology). Elegant designs are not only consistent and congruent with other organization systems, but they take advantage of the other systems and effectively use the leverage points to achieve the purposes of the system.

Steps

Identify key inputs, outputs, and interconnections and relationships with other internal and external systems. You must also identify key internal and external inputs to the system. For example, key inputs into a strategic management system might include trends in society, the environment, etc., assessment of the competitive environment, results (trends and comparisons) for the main aspects of the organization, and sustainability issues.

Identify key system or process outputs. For example, key outputs of a strategic management system might include goals and objectives, performance measures and targets, time horizons, environmental scan results, and action plans. In addition, most organization systems include flows of information to, through, and from the system being designed. The linkages between the information and communication systems is an important consideration and can change what is possible with the new design.

Example Leadership System

The leadership system is supported by and integrated with several other major management systems including: strategic management system, information and analysis system, customer and stakeholder knowledge system, operations system, human resource system, the enterprise scorecard, performance review system, and the governance system. As one CEO noted, "The first thing, I think you've got to see the connectivity in these things. I think you got to be a systems thinker so that you see that if I push in here it's going to push out somewhere else, so these things are related, and you got to see them as a system."

The nine elements of the leadership system presented here in Chapters 2 through 10 are all inter-connected with their larger system. For the details, see the section titled "Align and Integrate" near the end of each of those chapters. The leadership system at the upper echelon is directly linked to the strategy development and deployment systems. In fact, some CEOs have difficulty separating the leadership system from the strategic management system. As one CEO noted, "In fact for me I don't think you can really separate category 1 [Leadership] and category 2 [Strategic Planning] because to me they are so closely intertwined that I pretty much view them as the leadership process for us."

One of the areas often missed by the design team is the linkage to and congruence with the compensation and incentives systems. Incentives can be powerful influences on human behavior but are often at odds with the overall direction of the organization. Successful implementation and sustainability of the new design are dependent on the design of the related human resource systems and in particular the incentive system. It is this discovery activity that has the biggest impact on the design team's ability to LEAP the maturity levels and develop an aligned and integrated design.

8. Diagnosis

The last step in the discovery phase is a diagnosis of the current system. Unfortunately, traditional organization systems assessments often focus solely on the technical effectiveness of the system. These assessments often fail to ask how the users and stakeholders experience the system. For example, many systems are designed to produce high-quality products and services at a reasonable cost. This somewhat technical approach often fails to assess the human dimensions of the system, including convenience for the users, creativity and innovation, and empowerment.

This lack of human-centered design often results in unintended consequences such as wasted time, demotivation, and reduce productivity. For example, inconvenient processes waste valuable employee time reducing productivity and increasing costs. Inconvenient processes send the message to the employees that their time isn't valuable to the organization. Convenient systems are easier to implement and increase the likelihood system deployment will be successful and sustainable.

Current System Description

It is very difficult to diagnose an existing system until the details and design of the system are made explicit. Participants describe the key characteristics of the existing system in sufficient detail to provide a common understanding for the diagnosis. There are two methods commonly used to make a system description explicit — a visual flowchart or concept diagram and a table detailing the specifics of the individual components in the diagram.

The challenge here is to stay out of the weeds. Design teams often lose their energy when they spend too much time in the details of an organization system that is not previously well-defined. A helicopter view of the main components of the managements system provides the system perspective and keeps the design team's energy high. The intent of this step is to capture the existing process without spending a lot of time if the existing process is not currently documented. Once explicit, the design team can assess how well the current design addresses the key criteria.

Assessment

To assess the current system design and identify strengths and opportunities for improvement, the design team answers seven questions.

1. How well does the current system fulfill the **purposes** and **requirements** identified in Discovery step 1?

2. How consistent is the current design with the **nature** of the system identified in Discovery step 2?

3. How consistent is the current design with the relevant **theories** and **concepts** identified in Discovery step 3?

4. How does the design compare to the **inspiring examples** identified in Discovery step 4?

5. How well does the current design fit and support the **unique context** of the organization identified in Discovery step 5?

6. How does the current design reflect the **design principles** identified in Discovery step 6?

7. How well is the current design **integrated** with the other related management systems identified in Discovery step 7?

The discovery phase should provide a springboard into the creative phase, but the diagnosis step can undermine the amount of spring the team gets going into the design phase. After spending so much time using their critical thinking skills during the diagnosis step, many design teams have difficulty making the shift to the creative activities of design and development.

9. Design

The design emerges from the development of multiple options to identify an ideal but doable system. Three versions of the design are developed in this phase including an ideal conceptual design, a doable conceptual design, and a detailed design. Using the information and concepts from the first eight steps as a springboard, the design team develops an ideal conceptual design.

Ideal Conceptual Design

During this first step, participants stretch their thinking to develop a vision of how the organization system being designed could work in an ideal world. In this case, an ideal world is defined as one with unlimited resources and technology as well as the desired ideal culture. This might at first seem like a wasted step. You might be thinking, why not just go directly to a doable design?

Experience suggests that if the participants first develop an ideal design with few constraints and then a doable design with constraints, they will end up with a better design than if they go directly to the doable design. When attempting to redesign a system or process, participants are often prisoners of their previous experiences and learning. Participants that attempt to go directly from the current design to the desirable but doable design, often fall well short of what is actually possible. The challenge is to stretch the team's thinking to develop a vision of how the organization could be in an ideal world.

Doable Conceptual Design

Once the participants have developed the ideal conceptual design, it is time to identify the constraints to achieving that design. Participants review the ideal design and identify the challenges and obstacles to developing and deploying the ideal design. Once the obstacles and challenges are identified, the participants use creativity exercises and techniques to develop solutions to overcome the constraints. Using the creative solutions identified for the constraints, the participants refine the ideal design to create a doable conceptual design. The challenge here is to go beyond choosing from a menu of existing design options and instead develop new and innovative ways to accomplish the purpose and requirements for the particular system. Sometimes constraints are tied directly to the design decisions that were made in the previous step. Consequently, we often have to go back and change the original ideal design and go a different direction. If the team can't figure out how to overcome or get rid of a constraint, they may have to make some compromises but that is usually a last resort. Once the doable conceptual design is complete, the team move on to develop the details.

Detailed Design

There are many ways to develop a detailed design. After identifying the various options from the example systems and processes, the design team then mixes and matches the individual components to create a new combination. Once the components are chosen, they are creatively adapted to the specific situation and system. Then the doable design informs the hard work of developing a detailed design that is then tested, refined, and deployed (implemented).

The last phase of a [re]design project is the full scale development of the detailed design, the deployment of the new system, and the continuous improvement of the new system.

Develop

Once the detailed design is complete, the development phase begins. Depending on the nature of the process, it might be useful to develop a prototype and test that design with a small group before full-scale implementation. This will allow the design team to learn from the limited deployment and refine the design before it is fully implemented. This is a common practice for systems and processes that have a major technology component (e.g., ERP systems). Once the new design has been fully developed and refined to meet the feasibility criteria, it is ready for full-scale implementation. To fully develop the new system, the design team must work with all the "owners" of the integration points throughout the organization. While easier said than done, involving them in the process helps smooth the inevitable rough patches of deployment.

Deploy

Deploying a system or process throughout the appropriate parts of the organization is an exercise in leading change. Successful full-scale implementation of a new design requires a plan, trained employees, resources, and a process to review progress. The first step is to plan the implementation of the new design. This plan should include key activities, a timeline, and the resources required. In addition, the workforce cannot execute the new or redesigned process unless they understand how it works. Of course, the easier it is to execute, the less training is required. Most new processes, however, require some level of training. Once deployed, continue to fully develop the system and processes as more groups in the organization use the process and identify areas for improvement.

Iterate

A periodic review process is needed to record progress and keep the implementation on track. High-performing systems and processes have learning loops built into them to ensure continuous innovation and improvement of the new system and to keep it current with changing stakeholder needs. These loops include systematic assessment and reflection on the system performance, leading to the development of improvement plans.

As changes are made to the design, each implemented change should be monitored and adjustments made if the anticipated results are not achieved. This is a never-ending process of continuous learning and improvement.

ALIGN AND INTEGRATE

The process of [re]design and the system designs are aligned and integrated with other systems throughout the organization.

Stakeholder Value - The needs of the stakeholder segments inform the design of the systems, products, and processes. In addition, understanding the needs of the stakeholders is Step 1 in the system [re]design framework described here in Chapter 6.

Compelling Directive - The mission and vision provide the overall picture of the ideal organization design and key design characteristics. It also guides organization [re]design decisions throughout the organization. The results from the [re]design initiative should contribute to accomplishing the mission and achieving the vision.

Focused Strategy - Goals and objectives drive the scope and requirements of the [re]design initiatives. The benefits and results that are produced by the new designs should contribute to the overall strategy. Progress toward the [re] design initiatives should equal progress toward the strategy.

Enable, Empower, Engage - The workforce is an input to the [re]design efforts as well as a beneficiary. Enabling, empowering, and engaging the workforce in [re] design efforts is critical to designs that serve the needs of the stakeholders AND the technical requirements. Well-designed systems also benefit the workforce, who have to execute many of those systems.

Comprehensive Scorecard - The scorecard provides indicators of the quality of the [re]design. In addition, it helps us validate changes in performance relative to design changes. Plus, it provides insights into the diagnosis of the current design.

Organization Performance Review - Performance reviews study the performance of the systems, and from the analysis and dialogue, the strategic initiatives and [re] design projects are refined.

Reinforce Behavior - Leaders reward system innovation and improvement. Leaders don't punish failure; they celebrate courage and creativity.

Learn and Improve - The [re]design process itself is an iterative learning process that contributes to the overall understanding of the organization. What is learned from other learning and improvement processes also informs and enhances the [re]design process.

LEADER AS ORGANIZATION ARCHITECT

Leaders are the lead designers of the organization. One of the reasons leaders must take on the mantle of lead designer is they are the only ones with formal power to change the organization systems. Although leaders may not be involved with designing all the details of systems, they serve as sponsors of goal deployment [re]design initiatives. Leaders establish the standards for excellence by setting and enforcing high but reasonable expectations.

Collaborative leaders involve and engage people in the development and deployment of [re]design action plans. Then they make sure people have what they need to do their jobs and execute the [re]design plans. Involved leaders consistently communicate the importance of follow-through and deployment. Finally, leaders as organization architects listen and learn from the lessons derived from the development, implementation, and management of action plans and operations.

REFLECTION QUESTIONS

Take a few moments to assess your systems just using the information you have in your head.

    Are your systems explicitly defined and does everyone know how their work contributes to the overall system?
    Do you systematically redesign your processes and systems to improve performance?
    If you were going to [re]design your systems, where would you start? Where is the greatest pain?

The [re]design of organization systems may be the biggest and most challenging task the organization architect faces as they lead the journey to sustainable excellence. [Re]Design requires thinking that is critical, creative, and multi-disciplinary. And it requires collaboration across many functions and levels in the organization. As design projects unfold and prototypes are tested, the scorecard provides the measures to help the design team understand the effectiveness of the design changes.

7

COMPREHENSIVE SCORECARD

INTRODUCTION

How do we know if the strategies and systems are creating value for multiple stakeholders? All too often, we find out too late that the strategy is not working, or the systems are not performing. When the customer opens a defective product, it is too late.

While it might be possible to delight the customer with your organization's ability to respond and fix the problem, it is doubtful that you have the processes to do that well if you can't get it right in the first place. Also, it is much more expensive to fix problems after delivery than it is to prevent problems. In some cases, the fix wipes out all of the profit and more.

Even more important, we need feedback as early as we can get it on how strategies are working so we can make adjustments. Not only do we need feedback as early in the process as possible, we need a deep understanding of how the system works so that we can understand what the early measures actually mean for downstream performance. A comprehensive scorecard goes beyond a simple bottom line to a deeper understanding of the organization as a system.

Three Integrated Perspectives

A comprehensive scorecard addresses the value for the stakeholders, the progress and effectiveness of the strategy, and the performance of the systems and processes throughout the organization. We start with the stakeholders because the purpose of the organization is to create value for the stakeholders. The strategy is second because it should be designed to increase value for the stakeholders.

A strategy is an untested hypothesis that we create. We use our current understanding of the external and internal factors to develop what we think will work best for our customers (patients, students, primary beneficiaries, etc.). However, until we implement the strategy, we don't really know if our hypothesis is correct. When it comes to organization strategy, the results of a hypothesis are seldom simply it worked or didn't work. The results are often mixed, but we can adjust our strategy to change the outcome if we have feedback early enough in the process.

Finally, we address the system last because "form follows function." While we address the development of these three perspectives in the order of stakeholders, strategy, and systems, we use the reverse order to identify performance measures for the scorecard.

There are many ways to organize a scorecard but the alignment between the stakeholders, strategy, and systems makes it easy to organize around the systems and still gain insights about the strategy and stakeholders. Systems measures include all the systems measures as well as those used for strategy and stakeholders. For example, customer satisfaction is an example of a measure that includes all three perspectives. First, it is an indicator of how well the organization system is working. Second, it is often an indicator of strategy performance. Strategy often includes goals and objectives focused on the improvement of customer satisfaction. Third, it is a stakeholder outcome and measure of how well we are doing with the customer stakeholder group.

While not all system measures are directly related to stakeholders or the strategy, all stakeholder and strategy measures are related to the system. Consequently, our approach here is to use the systems model as the framework to identify the scorecard.

Selection Criteria

As you identify each candidate measure, use the following selection criteria to determine whether to include or exclude it from your scorecard. For each proposed measure ask the following five questions in order.

1. Is this measure a Stakeholder or Regulatory Requirement? In other words, do we have to measure and report this regardless whether WE find it useful?

If "YES" then add it to the scorecard. If "NO" then see #2

2. Is the measure actionable? If we did measure it, could we take action on the results? Is it an indirect measure of something that is actionable? Does it validate other measures that are actionable? For example, customer satisfaction is often a lagging measure that occurs after we deliver our product or service. However, we can probably influence those things that determine customer satisfaction, such as on-time delivery. So customer satisfaction is indirectly actionable. The trick is to measure what is useful vs. what is simply easy to measure.

If the answer is "NO" then drop it. If "YES" then see #3, 4, 5.

If the answer to ANY ONE of the following is "YES," then

add the measure to the scorecard. If the answer to ALL three is "NO," then drop it.

3. **Systems** - Will it help us manage or improve a system in the organization?

4. **Strategy** - Will it help us develop or deploy the strategy?

5. **Stakeholders** - Will it help us understand or validate the value created for a stakeholder?

The main goal of the criteria is to eliminate those measures that will not provide value for the effort. Using the stakeholders, strategy, and systems as guides along with the selection process and criteria, identify the measures that you need to manage and improve organization performance.

DESIGNING THE SCORECARD

The top-level systems introduced in the previous chapter help guide the development of the top-level systems scorecard. As we identify the measures for each system component we consider the stakeholders, the strategy, and the system. While there is no one best way or sequence to develop a comprehensive scorecard, the following sequence has proven a useful starting point (Figure 7-1).

Figure 7-1 Comprehensive Scorecard

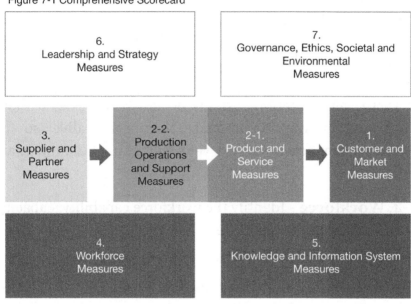

There are seven steps to a comprehensive scorecard. We begin by identifying the core value production systems measures.

1. **Customer** - We begin building the scorecard by identifying the measures for the stakeholders who receive, experience, and use the outputs (mission) of the organization.

2. **Production** - Working backward, we then identify the measurable characteristics of the products and services that predict customer success and satisfaction. Product and service quality and performance are lagging measures, so we also need to identify process measures that we can manage and adjust to produce quality outputs.

3. **Suppliers and Partners** - Identify the measures of incoming products and services that predict the operations and support process measures, which then predict products and services performance and ultimately customer satisfaction and success.

These value creation systems do not really exist without people and information to make them come alive, so the enabler system measures are developed that predict value chain performance.

4. **Workforce** - Identify the workforce capability, capacity, and engagement measures that predict the value chain performance and success.

5. **Knowledge and Information Systems** - Identify the knowledge and information system performance measures that reflect the knowledge and information system needs of the stakeholders.

The performance of the value creation and enabler systems is influenced by the guidance systems.

6. **Leadership + Strategy** - Identify the leadership measures, including the financial measures that reflect organization and leadership performance relative to the investors. In addition, identify the standard measurement dimensions for the deployment of strategic initiatives including scope, schedule, cost, and quality.

7. **Governance** - The last step is to identify the key governance measures, including ethics, social responsibility, and environmental sustainability.

These seven steps are a starting point, the design of a comprehensive scorecard is an iterative and often unpredictable process.

1. Customer and Market

The first step is to identify the measures that assess the outputs of the organization. Output measures include customer satisfaction and success. Customer satisfaction measures include perceptions (surveys, focus groups, complaints, etc.) and behaviors (sales, repeat business, referral purchases, etc.).

Customer Perceptions

We begin with perceptions. You have several options to collect feedback from customers. Focus groups and complaints offer qualitative information that can help you develop and improve your offerings. However, the analysis of qualitative data is limited. Customer surveys can scale perceptions of the customers on a variety of product and service characteristics from product usability to customer service representative tone and demeanor. The number and type of complaints can also be counted and converted to quantitative data. However, customer perceptions alone can provide limited and sometimes inaccurate insights.

Example Perception Measures
- Customer Perceived Value Survey
- Satisfaction with Customer Relationship Survey
- Overall Satisfaction % Top Box on Survey Scale
- Competitor Comparison Surveys

- Overall Dissatisfaction % Bottom Box on Survey Scale
- # Complaints by Type

Customer Behavior

Have you ever developed a product or service based on customer input such as focus groups, interviews, and feedback on current products, only to have them buy something else? Your first reaction might have been, "They lied to us." But the real explanation might be they just do not fully understand their own purchase decisions. That is why behavior is so important to validate customer feedback.

Purchase behavior and referrals tell us what the customer really thinks. First, are they coming back and spending more money with us? Repeat business is a solid indicator that the customer prefers us over the other options. Second, are they telling their friends and family about us? Referral business is the best kind of advertising regardless of the medium (e.g., word of mouth, social media).

The customer has to have a choice for repeat and referral business measures to be useful. If you have a monopoly or the customers are the recipient or primary beneficiaries of non-profit or government organization services, then these measures might not be available nor useful. However, you can measure customer success, which can be even better.

Example Behavior Measures

- % Repeat Purchase
- Total revenue from repeat purchases
- % Positive Referrals
- Total revenue from referral purchases
- Market Share
- New Markets Entered

Customer Success

For many organizations, the customer is using the product to solve a particular problem or accomplish a particular goal. The task here is to identify the measures of customer success. While you may not be able to control all the variables, measuring the degree to which your products or services were effective in helping the customer accomplish their goals is useful feedback and validation.

For example, in our earlier examples with education and healthcare, customer success depended upon the student and the patient's motivation, behavior, ability, etc. (See Chapter 2). Students who graduate but can't succeed in their chosen profession are not successful. Health-club customers who do not improve their fitness and health are not being successful. If you have a product or service that works, the customer will be able to use it to achieve their goals assuming that they do their part. Leaders run into resistance for measures such as this when we attempt to use them to evaluate the workforce. More on that in the next two chapters.

Example Customer Success Measures

Employer Evaluation (Survey)
% Hired in first six months after graduation
Weight lost
Blood Pressure Reduction
Tests passed
Golf Score Decrease # of Strokes

2. Production

Production measures include both the products and services produced and the processes that created them.

Products and Services

Feedback on the outcomes such as customer satisfaction and repeat and referral business is useful, but it is typically too late to help us manage the execution of the business. Consequently, we need product and service performance and quality measures that predict customer satisfaction. In other words, we need proxies for customer satisfaction. It is rare that all predictor measures have the same ability to predict customer satisfaction. Ideally we develop a panel of measures that are weighted based on the degree to which they influence customer satisfaction.

Examples

- % Defects
- % Returns / Refunds
- Warranty Work (repairs)
- % Replacements
- %Timely Delivery
- Customer Resolution Time
- Call Answer Speed
- # Abandoned Call

Operations and Support

Operations and support (product development, production, and delivery) measures **predict** product and service performance. In other words, they are "proxies" for product and service quality. This exercise can become a bit overwhelming if you don't control the scope.

Most organizations are a complex network of processes where the next operation is the customer. Consequently, there are many levels of internal processes with their own outputs leading to subsequent processes in the system. When developing the top-level scorecard, focus on the key production and support processes essential for producing the products and services that go to external customers. Later in your journey to sustainable excellence, you will have all parts of the organization develop their own measures for their particular value production system.

Examples

- Construction time each unit
- Cycle Time % Improvement
- Book to Ship Time Hours
- Process Improvements
- Inventory Turns
- Productivity
- Cost Reductions
- Patents Issued

3. Suppliers and Partners

The production processes are influenced by the quality of the incoming raw materials and supplies. The supplier and partner measures **predict** the production process results and, in turn, product and service performance and quality. For many organizations, supplier and partner performance goes beyond the quality of incoming raw materials. For some organizations, the production and delivery of products and services is accomplished through a partnership where both parties have a substantial influence on the overall product performance and customer satisfaction.

As with your organization's products and services, waiting until the end to measure quality can be an expensive way to ensure quality. Similarly, inspecting incoming materials can be an expensive and time-consuming way to ensure supplier quality. Consequently, some organizations have certified their suppliers' processes and outputs so they don't have to inspect each shipment. As one CEO noted, "We believed in long-term suppliers rather than firing them. We help them develop scorecards and work with them to develop the criteria for doing events together."

Examples

- # Preferred Suppliers
- Total # of Suppliers
- Rejection Rate (PPM)
- On-time Delivery
- Costs & Cost Reductions
- Product Reliability

4. Workforce

Systems without people don't exist. Even automated processes and systems are created, developed, maintained, and improved by people. In other words, people bring the processes and systems to life. Consequently, value chain performance is dependent on the dedicated efforts and performance of the workforce.

Humans are complex and unpredictable. After years of research we are still trying to improve how we develop and engage people to create great products, services, and customer experiences. Consequently, the workforce scorecard often includes a diverse array of measures that include many connections and relationships. Like customer satisfaction, workforce measures include both perceptions of the people and measures of actual performance, addressing well-being, development, and performance.

Examples

Employee Well-being and Satisfaction/ Dissatisfaction

- Employee Satisfaction and Engagement Survey
- Voluntary Turnover %
- Absenteeism # Days
- Accidents/100 Employees
- Injuries # Days Missed Work

Employee Development

- Courses completed
- % Cross-trained
- Training dollars per employee
- Training Hours/Employee

Work System Performance

- Innovation/Suggestion rates
- On-the-job Performance Improvements

5. Knowledge and Information Systems

Whether executing the process or developing automated digital systems, the workforce and leaders need knowledge and information to do their jobs. There are two types of measures for knowledge and information systems, including measure of the content and the system. Content measures focus on the amount and type of content, user perceptions, and the reliability of the data. System measures focus on the user experience and the reliability of the system. For some situations, the information system content, delivery, and reliability are part of the core production and delivery processes. In those situations, you will have to decide where to put the measures. Where measures are placed in the scorecard is not critical as long as the analysis of the relationships between measures is correct.

Examples

- # of Best Practices Included in Knowledge Database
- System Reliability % Uptime
- Knowledge System User Friendly Survey Score
- System User Satisfaction Survey Score
- % of Measures with Competitive Comparisons
- % of Measures with Industry or World Class Comparisons

6. Leadership + Strategy

While leaders are responsible for the whole organization and performance for all stakeholders, there are a few measures that are specific to their position, roles, and responsibilities. We begin with the leadership scorecard that defines role model leadership behavior. As one CEO said, "The key that I really found through all of this is the leadership scorecard was role model behavior, and so the scorecard defined what leaders do in our company . . . It defines what we felt role model leadership was at every level in the organization."

For many organizations, this involves where leaders spend their time. Another CEO noted, "We had a saying, your priority is where your feet are and the leadership scorecard measured all the aspects of leadership and literally gave you a grade." For example, leadership scorecards often track how many hours leaders spend with stakeholders. This often includes spending time with customers — sometimes in person and sometimes monitoring the customer-care line.

Leadership behavior has a substantial impact on workforce satisfaction and thus getting the right scorecard for leaders is critical to developing a sustainable culture of service and excellence. While one might make the case that all the metrics are a result of leadership, a leadership scorecard that includes measures that are direct and controllable by leaders can be useful predictors of overall organization performance, including financial performance.

Financial

Leaders are the agents for the investors whether they are owners, donors, or taxpayers. Consequently, leaders are responsible for the financial performance of the organization — both growing the revenue and controlling expenses to create the most value for the least cost. The goal of commercial investors is the biggest return on their investment for a certain amount of risk.

There has been quite a bit of criticism bemoaning the short-term focus of stockholders and markets and how they often trade the long-term success of the firm for short-term gains. It is interesting to note that many of the organizations that are successful transforming their companies to achieve sustainable excellence are privately held. There could be many explanations for this, but owners of privately held, high-performing companies often describe their motivations as the long-term economic viability of the firm and a legacy of an economic engine for their heirs.

Non-profit investors or donors generally want their donations to have the greatest impact on the primary beneficiaries (e.g., hungry children). Leaders are interested in attracting even more donations and thus are responsible for creating an organization that is the as effective as it can be at operating, producing, and serving their beneficiaries.

Consequently, the financial focus of non-profit organization is often on the overhead burden or reducing expenses related to serving the primary beneficiaries. Government employees, political appointees, and elected officials are stewards of taxpayer monies and responsible for creating an organization that accomplishes their mandated mission for the least amount of tax burden. Regardless of the type of organization, financial measures address both income and expenses to assess the effective use of money from investors, donors, or taxpayers.

Examples

- Revenue
- Profitability
- Return on Sales (ROS) % Improvement
- Return on Net Assets (RONA) % Improvement
- Operating Margins
- Liquidity
- Debt to Equity Ratio
- Net Asset Turnover
- Cost of Quality
- Unit Cost
- Days Cash On Hand

Strategy

There are two dimensions to the strategy scorecard. First

there are the measures that are associated with the goals and objectives identified in the strategy (See Chapter 4). The measures associated with the goals and objectives track the performance improvements resulting from the [re]design, development, and deployment of organization systems. Next, there are the measures used to track and manage the strategic initiatives and projects. Strategic initiatives are tracked using four types of measures: performance or quality, schedule, cost, and scope.

The first measure is the quality or performance of the new organization system design. For most projects, the quality requirements are held constant while the design team manages the three other constraints. The schedule is the second most common metric used to track progress. Is the project unfolding in the time expected? The third metric is the cost - both operating and capital expenses. Operating cost includes the level of effort (hours) spent by the members on the project. Finally, the scope of the project is tracked to keep the project within the planned parameters and to force conscious changes to scope based on the other three progress measures.

Schedule, cost, and scope are all inter-related and when one changes the other two are impacted. Consequently, leaders need all four metrics to effectively track and manage the design project.

7. Governance Ethics Social and Environmental

The last area of the scorecard measures the governance, ethics, regulatory, social responsibility, and sustainability efforts of the organization. While these measures may not be the primary purpose of the firm, they are indicators of how well the systems are addressing the needs of key stakeholders including investors, society, and the natural environment. The challenge is to operate the firm and create products that are economically viable for the investors, avoid ethical dilemmas, meet or exceed regulations, and are good for society and the natural environment.

Given our current measurement and understanding of systems, it isn't always clear how ethical concerns contribute to or predict the financial success or upside. We need more measures and better analysis to fully appreciate the connections. However, the risks are very clear and missteps in any one of these areas could cause you to lose the entire firm. Note - excellence is about role model performance, not simply meeting requirements.

Examples

Legal, Regulatory and Ethics
- Penalties and Fines $
- # Audit Findings by Type
- # Ethic Hotline Calls
- # Conformed Ethics Violations by Type)

Community
- Charity Contributions $/Employee
- Avg. Volunteer Hours/Employee
- # Charity Events Sponsored

Environment
- Recycling $$
- Annual Paper Recycling Tons
- Waste
- Energy Use Reductions

- VOM Emissions/Sale
- GHG/CO_2 Emissions gross; Less: Sequestration = GHG/CO_2 emissions net

Whole Organization or Just a Piece?

While we discuss the scorecard development from the perspective of the top-level and the entire organization, it is equally applicable to a department or part of the organization. As you move down into the various departments in the organization, each has their own version of these seven areas. Some areas within a lower level may include the exact same measures as the level above and some areas may have measures unique to their area that predict the performance of the of the area(s) above. For example, the output measures at lower levels might be the in-process measures in the main production process at the upper-levels. At the same time, the workforce satisfaction measures might be the same throughout the organization. It takes time and typically multiple iterations to develop a comprehensive scorecard at any level.

Iterative Process

While we have discussed the identification of scorecard measures in a linear sequence, the actual process is less predictable and iterative. I have never seen an organization develop a top-level scorecard in one sitting. It always takes time to identify measures, collect data, and test their ability to provide insights and predict performance. The trick is to create the best first draft version possible, then begin implementing the measures and adjust as you go. When developing the scorecard measures, you also need to define the data collection and display requirements.

DIMENSIONS OF PERFORMANCE
AND PROGRESS

To understand the performance of the system, one has to collect and display data so that it addresses three dimensions for each measure — current level of performance, trend over time, and comparison to other organizations. First, the data must show the current level of performance. How good is the organization performing today? This can be expressed in a variety of ways, including a percentage, an actual performance level, an average performance level, etc. The operational definition has to be clear and consistent so that you can track trends over time and compare the levels and trends with other organizations. Second, we need to know the trend. Is the level of performance improving and at what rate? Third, how does the current level and the trend over time compare to other comparable organizations (e.g., competitors)? Comparisons combine both the level of performance and the trends.

Figure 7-2 Your Organization Improving Faster Than Comparison

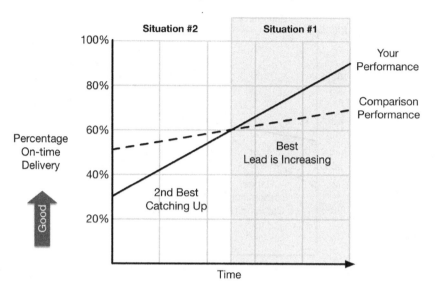

Measuring performance and comparing your organization's performance to other high-performing organizations can help create dissatisfaction with the status quo: a key part of creating the tension needed to overcome the inertia of the status quo.

When comparing performance there are two basic situations — either you are learning (improving) faster than the competition or the competition is learning (improving) faster than you.

The best situation is when you are learning faster than the competition, and you are already ahead of the competition and gaining ground — increasing the lead (Situation #1 - Figure 7-2). The second-best situation is you are learning faster than the competition, but they are currently better than you, though you are catching up (Situation #2 - Figure 7-2).

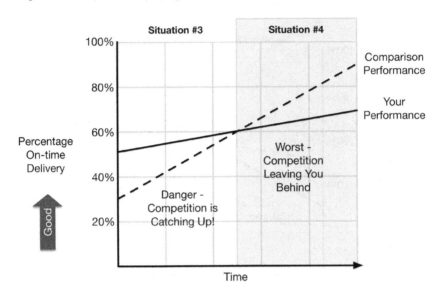

Figure 7-3 Comparison Improving Faster Than Your Organization

If the comparison organization is behind but learning faster than you are (Situation #3 – Figure 7-3), then it is only a matter of time until they are ahead (Situation #4 – Figure 7-3), and leaving you behind. The only way to address the comparison issue is to figure out how to learn faster than the comparison organizations.

ALIGN AND INTEGRATE

Stakeholder Value - Stakeholder segmentation informs the selection of the measures included in the scorecard. Each stakeholder group and segment is measured in the comprehensive scorecard. In addition, the specific needs of each segment inform the development of predictor measures such as product and service quality measures. For a full description of stakeholder groups see Chapter 1.

Compelling Directive - The comprehensive scorecard includes measures (direct and indirect) of performance relative to the mission today and progress toward the vision of tomorrow.

Focused Strategy - The comprehensive scorecard includes measures of the outcomes described in the strategic goals and objectives. The scorecard also includes measures of progress toward the strategy such as [re]design project cost, quality, schedule, and scope.

Enable, Empower, Engage - The comprehensive scorecard includes a group of indicators that measure multiple dimensions of the workforce, including their capability, capacity, level of engagement, etc. The indicators provide information on the success of enable, empower, and engage efforts and help identify areas for improvement.

[Re]Design Systems - The scorecard measures the performance and progress of the [re]design project. In addition, it helps us validate changes in performance relative to design changes. It also provides insights into the diagnosis of the current design.

Organization Performance Review - It might be obvious, but we can't review and analyze results that we don't measure or data that we don't collect. The scorecard provides the results for the organization performance review. What we learn from these reviews also informs the further development and refinement of the scorecard.

Reinforce Behavior - We reinforce achievement of the desired results, but we do not limit recognition to those things that can be measured quantitatively.

Learn and Improve - Learning and improvement processes rely on several fact-based inputs, including the results measured by the comprehensive scorecard.

LEADER AS ORGANIZATION ARCHITECT

Organization architects of sustainable excellence lead the development and implementation of a comprehensive scorecard to measure stakeholders, strategy, and systems. While this has to be done at the top to measure overall organization performance, it is also needed at all levels of the organization. Leaders at each level in the organization have to lead the development of scorecards for their particular part of the organization. Organization architects are motivated to work with facts and knowledge and always seem to want to know more. Successful leaders involve stakeholders to develop and test the key performance measures for the enterprise system. Also, leaders measure their own performance by including measures of the desired leadership style in the annual employee survey. Finally, leaders push the continuous development and refinement of the enterprise scorecard to support system understanding and fact-based management from the top of the organization to the bottom.

REFLECTION QUESTIONS

Ask yourself these four questions to assess your overall scorecard.

Does your scorecard address all your **stakeholders**? If not, who and what is missing?

Does your scorecard measure progress on toward your **strategy**?

Does your scorecard measure all key aspects of **system** performance? If not, what is missing?

Does your scorecard include **comparisons** to relevant organizations, benchmarks, and standards?

Measurement by itself is a parasite. It consumes valuable organization resources, and thus should provide more value that it consumes. Consequently, measures should help leaders run the organization or improve the organization, or they are not worth the cost of measuring. So how do you come up with the candidate measures?

There are three main sources of measures: stakeholder feedback, system performance, and progress on the strategy. While in this book we addressed the system measures in sequence, in reality it is often an iterative process and proposed measures can emerge from any of the sources at any time. Eventually, the comprehensive scorecard includes measures of all three perspectives or cornerstones: stakeholders, strategy, and systems. These measures are aggregated and delivered for analysis and review during regular organization performance reviews.

8

ORGANIZATION PERFORMANCE REVIEW

INTRODUCTION

Now that we have the four cornerstones of stakeholders, strategy, systems, and scorecard in place, we are ready to use them as the framework for periodic organization performance reviews.

We often treat the strategy as a realistic plan, when in fact it is simply a hypothesis. As one CEO noted, "So you got to follow through — you can't just be a visionary. I used to think people would naturally follow me; I was wrong. I used to think I'll just communicate, and they will all jump in there and make it happen. That didn't happen." Once you develop the strategy and conduct the strategy deployment experiment and measure the results, you are ready to study those results and learn what worked, what didn't work, and under what conditions.

Periodic organization performance reviews serve two purposes. First, they help leaders track performance and progress and make adjustments to keep the organization on track. Some refer to this as single-loop learning. Second, they provide learning opportunities to better understand the organization system and make changes to the underlying design of the systems. Some refer to this as double-loop learning. The organization performance review process consists of four phases: alignment of inputs, analysis, dialogue and decisions, and follow-through (Figure 8-1).

Figure 8-1 Organization Performance Review Process

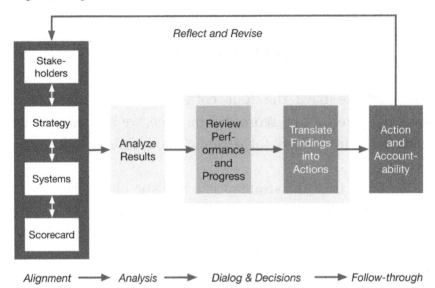

The review process begins by aligning the four cornerstone inputs in preparation for analysis. Then behind the scenes analysis is conducted in preparation for the leadership dialogue. During the dialogue, the analyzed inputs are reviewed and specific issues analyzed by the cross-functional leadership team. Decisions are made to adjust the plan and sometimes the system design. To ensure these decisions are implemented, clear accountability is identified with a follow-up schedule to review and revise.

ALIGNMENT

The first phase of the organization performance review (OPR) process is the alignment of the inputs including stakeholders, strategy, systems, and the scorecard. Each of the four cornerstones provides a piece of the puzzle and helps clarify the meaning of the individual results. There are three basic types of measures: the performance of the organization system, the progress on the strategy, and the value that is created for the six stakeholder groups.

We use the systems perspective as the foundation, then identify the strategic goals and stakeholders associated with the systems. The reason for using the system as the integrating perspective is that all measures are related to systems but not all measures are associated directly with strategy or stakeholders. The second reason we focus on systems is that they are what we change in order to get different results. So the direct relationship between action and results is found in the linkages between the systems and scorecard. The linkages between the four cornerstones inform the analysis and the dialogue to facilitate a deep understanding of the causes and outcomes related to the measures.

In short, alignment makes the connections between the performance from the scorecard with the systems, strategy, and stakeholders explicit. This helps increase clarity between actions and results. With this solid foundation, the next phase is the analysis of the results.

ANALYSIS

The technical analysis of the results is completed before the review meeting. This allows for a more thorough treatment of the data and the linkages. Also, the analysis before the meeting allows for further research into areas that are not performing as planned to make sure additional data and information are gathered, analyzed, and prepared for the review meeting. Analyzing organization performance often requires a wide variety of methods, tools, and techniques.

Analysis methods can range from stoplight charts to visual

displays of descriptive statistics to more advanced methods including regression and structural equation modeling (SEM). Each method offers different insights, so we often use several types of analysis for a single aspect of the organization. The analysis also provides a way to triage a prioritized review meeting agenda. Leadership teams seldom have the time to dive into all the measures and analysis that are included in the regular measurement and analysis of organization performance. The analysis includes both the organization performance and the progress on strategy deployment, each with their own methods and stoplight systems.

Organization Performance

Analyzing organization performance includes a review of each individual measure and their relationships to other measures. We begin by reviewing the level, trend, and comparisons for each individual result. This review requires clear, unambiguous definitions for the stoplight categories and then an analysis of the three dimensions together. The second phase of organization performance is an analysis of the relationships between the results. This is first accomplished visually and through discussion, then through statistical modeling as appropriate. We begin with stoplight chart with color codes that help identify the areas that deserve discussion.

Stoplight Definitions

A stoplight approach categorizes the results into three (or more) categories (Figure 8-2). Stoplight charts summarize the status of the measures using the three lights in a stoplight including stop (red — poor), caution (yellow — low), and go (green — good to excellent). Note: Some organizations include a separate fourth level and color for excellent performance. The stoplight categories are included for all three dimensions of each measure: (1) level of performance, (2) trend (favorable, flat, or unfavorable), and (3) comparison to relevant organizations.

For each measure, the actual levels that are included in each category must be operationally defined. Once this is done, the data can be coded into the spreadsheet or data system so that it automatically color codes the results. The same can be done for the trend based on the previous data points and whether they are higher, the same, or lower. Finally, the comparison can be done based on three possible situations.

Figure 8-2 Stop Light Definitions - Performance

	Level	Trend	Comparison
Good (Green)	Level of performance is equal to or slightly better than the target.	Trend is favorable.	Improving faster than comparison but performance may not be not as good as comparison.
Low (Yellow)	Level of Performance is slightly less than the target.	Trend is flat.	Performance better than comparison but they are improving faster and catching up.
Poor (Red)	Level of performance is considerably lower than the target.	Trend is unfavorable.	Performance not as good as comparison and they are improving faster and the gap is getting wider.

Comparison Situation #1 - If you are improving faster than the comparison then the stoplight is "GREEN." If you are improving faster and but not quite as good as the comparison, you are on the right track and the action is to keep doing what you are doing. The same action is needed if you are better than the comparison and improving faster. Both situations are classified as green.

Comparison Situation #2 - If the comparison is not as good as your organization is today, but is improving faster than your organization, then it is only a matter of time until they are ahead and leaving you behind. This situation is YELLOW for caution — some action is needed to prevent being overtaken by the comparison. The only way to address this situation is to learn how to learn faster than the comparisons.

Comparison Situation #3 - If you are not as good as the comparison and the comparison is improving faster than you are, then this is the DANGER situation color coded "RED" In this last situation, action is needed to turn performance around and catch up.

The three dimensions — level, trend, and comparison — are analyzed together.

Stoplight Scenarios

The pattern of the three lights (level, trend, comparison) tells a story about the individual metric (Figure 8-3). For example, the level might be good, but the trend is unfavorable, and the performance compared to other organizations is getting worse. If we only pay attention to the level, we would miss the impending trouble. In fact, in some instances, the level and trend could be good, but the comparison (competitors) might be learning at a faster pace and catching up with you. In this case, the level and trend could give a false sense of security if you don't include the comparison (level and trend).

Figure 8-3 Stop Light Scenarios - Selected Performance Examples

Level	Trend	Comparison	Remarks
Good (Green)	Low (Yellow)	Low (Yellow)	Level is good: equal to or better than the target. However, trend is flat and the comparison is catching up. Need to start improving and at a rate faster than the competition.
Good (Green)	Good (Green)	Low (Yellow)	Level is good and improving. However, the comparison is improving faster and catching up. Need to learn and improve at an even faster rate.
Poor (Red)	Low (Yellow)	Poor (Red)	Level is below the target and the trend is flat while the comparison is ahead and leaving you behind. Intervention is required to turn this around and if that isn't possible consider outsourcing.
Low (Yellow)	Good (Green)	Low (Yellow)	Current level is slightly below target but the trend is favorable. Unfortunately, the comparison is improving at a faster pace and will soon catch up.

The stoplight method is a good starting point, but it doesn't help with relationships between the measures.

Systems Diagrams

All too often organizations create hierarchies of metrics where the lower levels are rolled up into higher level metrics. While this can be useful, it does not provide any insights into the performance of the organization as a system. A systems diagram with an overlay of stoplight results can illuminate the linkages between the various components of the system. The visual display of performance with the explicit linkages between the measures facilitates the identification of root causes.

While poor performance is sometimes limited to a single part of the system, often poor performance in one area impacts performance in subsequent or downstream operations. The visual display of the system with these performance levels provides the structure for tracing the poor performance trends back to their source. This informs action plans that address root causes vs. merely treating the symptoms.

Systems Scenario

The scenario depicted in the diagram (Figure 8-4) is a situation where root causes back in the system are causing undesirable results downstream (symptoms). In addition, these downstream symptoms are causing even further problems with the root causes.

Figure 8-4 Stop Light Results - A Systems Perspective

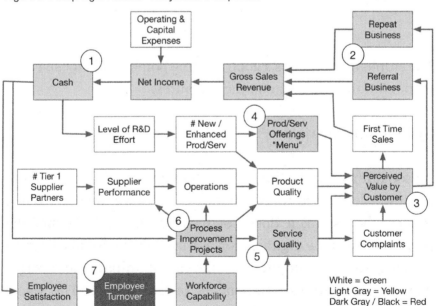

1. We begin with the low performance of the financials including sales, net income, and cash.

2. If we follow the trail backward, we find that repeat and referral business is below the target.

3. If we continue backward, we find that a likely explanation is the low performance of the customer-perceived value measure.

It seems that the perceived value is sufficient for first time sales, but once they experience the product and service, they do not buy again or tell their friends. Continuing our analysis, we find that there are two potential explanations for the low perceived value — low performance on the offerings menu (4) and low-service quality (5)

4. While the offering menu is low, the research and development and new and enhanced products are performing well. So it looks like this issue is in the process of being remedied.

5. However, if we look at the service quality there are two issues — one is the low performance on process improvement projects (PIP) (6) and the other is low workforce capability and capacity (7) which is also negatively influencing the low PIP performance.

6. Process improvement projects are not performing up to expectations. There could be several explanations including the workforce capability might be causing both the PIP (6) low performance and the low service quality (5).

7. Workforce capability and capacity is negatively impacted by the poor performance on employee turnover, which is influenced by employee satisfaction. This is the potential root cause for the downstream performance issues.

Given this analysis, our theory (explanation) of the situation might be low employee satisfaction is causing high turnover, which is negatively impacting workforce capability and capacity, and in turn, service quality and the projects to improve service quality. Low service quality is negatively influencing the perceived value by the customer, which is negatively impacting the repeat and referral purchases thus negatively impacting total sales, net income, and cash. To make matter worse, the low cash available is limiting our ability to resolve the issues with the workforce, making it worse. The reinforcing loop continues to get worse and worse in a downward spiral. The leverage point to turn this around appears to be employee satisfaction.

Statistical Analysis

While visual analysis of results is useful and often the best way to get a cross-functional group to understand the overall system, sometime statistical analysis is needed to fully understand and validate the system.

Historically, statistical modeling was only done by the most highly capitalized firms and the government. Why? The resources to collect the data and then conduct the analysis were so great that most small to mid-size firms and non-profit organizations couldn't afford them. While there are still barriers to this type of analysis, those barriers are coming down as we move toward more digital systems.

Digital systems are enabling the collection of data at very low and sometimes no cost once the system is designed. If you have a visual model of the system, and the processes are digital, you may be able to capture the necessary data for low cost but powerful analysis. However, the promise of Big Data will continue to elude many organizations until they develop a theory of the business with an explicit system model.

Modern organizations have many systems and processes that are continuously repeated. These value creation activities produce a variety of results that are analyzed and reviewed as part of the OPR. The OPR process often results in single-loop learning opportunities where adjustments are made to keep the organization on track. However, the OPR process also produces opportunities for double-loop learning based on analysis of the system relationships and longitudinal patterns of performance. In addition to organization performance, the OPR also provides learning opportunities for each strategic initiative project.

Strategy Deployment Progress

A formal review of the progress on strategic initiatives is an integral part of the organization performance review. The review and revision of key initiatives helps to keep the transformation on track and helps ensure the projects are achieving the desired results. While priorities and clear objectives at the top are critical to successful change, the initiatives that support these objectives must be a priority on the agendas of regularly scheduled and frequent senior management forums to ensure actual implementation. Like the organization performance review, the strategy progress review includes a stoplight system to help develop the review agenda and facilitate the discussion.

Stoplight Definitions

There are four dimensions of project management: the quality or success of the project, the schedule, the cost, and the scope. Each of these dimensions is rated on a three-point scale: green, yellow, red (Figure 8-5).

The quality dimension is the definition of success for the project. When the project is planned, the objective and how it will contribute to the strategy is described. That becomes the definition of project quality. It is rated on a scale from "meeting most requirements and expectations" to "it will meet some to many requirements and expectations" to "it will not meet many to most expectations" (See Figure 8-5).

The schedule dimension is based on how well the project is on the "revised" schedule. Schedules are often adjusted and changed during the life of the project so it doesn't help the review if we compare the current performance to the original schedule. The schedule is rated from "on revised schedule" to

Figure 8-5 Stop Light Definitions - Project

	Schedule	Scope	Cost	Quality - Performance
Good (Green)	On Revised Schedule	As Revised	On Track	Will meeting most requirements
Low (Yellow)	Revised Schedule @ Risk	Some Refinement Required	Slightly more than planned	Won't meet some expectations
Poor (Red)	Behind Revised Schedule	Major Refinement Required	Much more than planned	Won't meet many expectations

"revised schedule is at risk" to "behind revised schedule" (See Figure 8-5).

The cost dimensions which include manpower is set (estimated) at the beginning of the project. It is rated as "on track" to "slightly more than planned" to "much more than planned" (See Figure 8-5). Usually a specific % percent over budget is identified to define "slightly" and "much more."

The last dimension is scope of the project, which is essentially the amount of work or features and functions in the final product or completed project. Scope is sometimes revised during the life of the project and often increased as new ideas emerge and additional requirements identified. This "scope creep" is a common problem, as executives often have many more ideas than resources and the project team is left trying to meet the increased scope with the same quality, schedule, and cost. The rating for the stoplight system is based on the changes that have been made to the scope since the last adjustment (See Figure 8-5).

Stop Light Scenarios

The four dimensions of project management — quality (success), schedule, cost, and scope — are all inter-related. In other words, when we make changes to one, the others will change (Figure 8-6). In most cases, we attempt to hold quality or the definition of success constant. If we are behind schedule and want to stick to our original definition of success, we will either have to accept the later schedule OR add more resources to finish on time. We could reduce the scope but that usually impacts the quality or success.

Figure 8-6 Stop Light Scenarios - Selected Project Examples

Schedule	Scope	Cost	Quality - Perf	Remarks
Poor (Red)	Good (Green)	Good (Green)	Good (Green)	Way behind schedule. Option 1 - decrease the scope to get back on schedule. Option 2 - increase the cost by adding additional resources to the project. Option 3 - reset the schedule to reflect the current situation.
Good (Green)	Poor (Red)	Good (Green)	Good (Green)	Scope is out of control. However, everything seems to be on track so the project team is handling the additional scope. While everything is going well now, the additional scope could cause issues later in the project. Think through the longer-term implications and consider resetting the scope of the project.
Good (Green)	Good (Green)	Poor (Red)	Good (Green)	The project is on time, with good quality and scope but it is costing more than expected to achieve these results. Option 1 – reduce the cost and accept a change in the schedule. Option 2 – Reduce the scope of the project. Option 3 – Reset the budget to reflect the actual costs.
Low (Yellow)	Low (Yellow)	Good (Green)	Low (Yellow)	The good news is we are within budget. The bad news is we are behind, the scope is out of control and the quality and performance of the solution is suffering. The likely cause here is an increase in scope without a comparable increase in cost. Need to make a choice.

The analyzed results from the comprehensive scorecard, aligned with the strategy and systems, form a package for periodic analysis and review by the leadership team.

Learning

Every project offers new opportunities for learning and improvement. Projects by their nature vary in scope, schedule, cost, and quality requirements. While we do our best to estimate these dimensions as accurately as we can during the planning phase, there are often many opportunities for adjustment during the implementation of the project. In addition, projects are designed to produce specific results and outcomes. A new initiative is a hypothesis — if we do this, then we expect to get a specific result. Sometimes we are correct, and sometimes the project doesn't produce the results we predicted. Both progress and performance provide opportunities for learning and improvement.

DIALOG AND DECISIONS

The actual review of the organization's performance and progress is a process of review, dialogue, and decisions. For our purposes, we define dialogue as an open, frank, and professional interchange of ideas with the purpose of seeking meaning and greater understanding to maximize individual and team or organizational learning.

To ensure the open and frank exchange of ideas, the organization performance review (OPR) process needs to be one where the participants can explore ideas, no matter how out of the box they may be, without the fear of being attacked or put down. In other words, a safe place.

The leader's job is to role-model respect for people, facilitate a collaborative approach, and set the tone and norms of behavior for the reviews. This does not mean that team members do not challenge the ideas presented, for that is the essence of a frank and rich dialogue. It does mean that when they challenge ideas, they do it in a manner that does not demean the individual, and they do it in the spirit of trying to understand. This requires a balance of advocacy and inquiry.

Balancing Inquiry and Advocacy

Aircraft accident trends have decreased since the 1940s, primarily due to advancements in the technology and the reliability of airplanes and engines. However, accidents due to flight crew error have not decreased at the same rate. The root cause? Problem solving in the multi-place cockpit was not as effective as it could be.

In fact, post-accident investigation has often revealed that someone on the crew did have the right answer to the problem — but for some reason, usually team dynamics, that solution did not get implemented. Some airlines started programs to teach crews to effectively solve problems in the high-paced stressful environment of the modern cockpit. One of the keys to effective problems solving was the ability of the crew members to balance advocacy and inquiry. Effective team members advocate their ideas but at the same time they are humble and inquire into the ideas of others. The result is an exchange of ideas that include both creativity and critique.

Translate Findings Into Actions

Findings from the reviews are translated into actions for new initiatives or revisions to existing initiatives. While much of the learning during these reviews is limited to single-loop learning, occasionally the dialogue will result in an examination of the underlying assumptions and double-loop learning. Single-loop learning typically translates into refinements of how the project or process is being implemented. Occasionally, double-loop learning will require the examination of the underlying assumptions and system or solution design. Classifying the type of learning as single- or double-loop is not important. What is important is knowing when to move beyond single-loop learning and simply addressing the symptoms to double-loop learning and fundamentally changing the design.

FOLLOW-THROUGH

There is an old saying, "What gets measured gets done." But that is only true if someone with authority asks to see those measures and the progress on the action plans. All the alignment, analysis, and dialogue won't make a difference if you don't follow-through and make the changes necessary to achieve the desired performance.

Successful follow-through requires a systematic approach that ensures the changes are actually made and are reviewed at subsequent OPRs. As one CEO described, "We would report out on how we were actually performing in relationship to that plan that we had submitted the prior fall. So there was really accountability in place from a corporate perspective and ... of course, we tracked the results every month and so on." While periodic OPRs are essential, ongoing reflect and revise cycles are necessary between formal reviews to keep everything moving and responsive to the dynamic world we live in.

ALIGN AND INTEGRATE

Stakeholder Value - The stakeholder segments and needs combined with an understanding of the stakeholder system of service inform the analysis of the comprehensive scorecard results. In addition, the results of the review discussions inform the refinement of stakeholder segments and needs along with our understanding of the system.

Compelling Directive - While the organization performance reviews focus on the stakeholders, strategy, and systems, the mission and vision provide a touchstone for decision-making and refinements to the plans and processes.

Focused Strategy - The strategy is one of three critical dimensions of measurement and review. The dialogue on strategy includes both the improvements that the strategic initiatives have produced AND the progress and performance of individual projects (e.g., cost, quality, schedule, and cost).

Enable, Empower, Engage - Results related to the workforce are part of the organization performance review. But the most important aspect is the learning that takes place during the reviews helps enable, empower, and engage the leadership team and those they lead. As leaders, they are better equipped to provide clear expectations and direction.

[Re]Design Systems - Performance reviews study the performance of the systems and, based on the dialogue, the [re]design projects are refined to improve performance or new plans are developed and deployed.

Comprehensive Scorecard - We can't review and analyze results that we don't measure or data that we don't collect. The scorecard provides results for the organization performance review. What we learn from these reviews also informs further development and refinement of the scorecard.

Reinforce Behavior - Review results inform the recognition and rewards process. The results of the organization performance reviews identify those things that deserve recognition both successes and prudent failures.

Learn and Improve - Results of the organization performance review process inform the reflection, learn-ing, and improvement processes. The learning and improvement processes take the next step and go deeper into the analysis and learning required to make substantive changes to the organization.

LEADER AS ORGANIZATION ARCHITECT

Organization architects role-model the desired behaviors, balancing advocacy and inquiry to facilitate dialogue and learning during the organization review process. Demonstrable respect for individuals encourages frank, two-way dialogue, which is necessary for open and honest organization performance reviews. Organization performance reviews are conducted as a collaborative cross-functional group, resulting in a rich team dialogue and a deeper collective understanding of the system.

Effective leaders of transformation have the tenacity and patience to develop a team culture that approaches organization performance reviews as an enterprise group vs. a collection of functions. The group analyzes the enterprise system relationships between the measures to gain insights and identify leverage points to improve performance.

Leaders of sustainable excellence are personally involved and provide coaching during the organization review process. Finally, leaders are reflective and take the time to learn from the organization performance review process and use those lessons to improve organization performance.

REFLECTION QUESTIONS

Four questions about performance reviews and learning.

During your organization performance reviews do you go beyond reacting to symptoms and explore the underlying causes of the performance?

Are the findings from your organization performance reviews translated into revised or new initiatives and action plans?

What have you learned from your strategic initiatives and projects?

What have you learned about what makes your organization work best?

It may seem obvious, but we have more data today than ever before in history and it is in a digital form that can be manipulated like never before. However, the unfulfilled promise of Big Data is that is has yet to provide the insights we really need to create value for the multiple stakeholders. The combination of a systems model and a scorecard based on that model may help us leverage big data in a way that has eluded us up to this point. With more explicit systems and theories of how those systems work, we may be able to truly test the long-term, downstream results of the changes that we make to those systems. The organization performance review is the first of three learning components in the leadership system. Individual learning and overall organizational learning and improvement are addressed in the next two chapters, 9 and 10.

9

ALIGN, COACH, APPRECIATE

INTRODUCTION

Leaders are in charge of the incentives in the organization, and thus get exactly the performance from the people they deserve. All too often, the incentive systems are counter-productive and drive behaviors that are inconsistent with the overall compelling directive, strategy, and desired culture.

Reinforcement and incentives come in a wide variety of shapes, sizes, and degrees of formality. The formal options for reinforcing the desired behaviors include recognition, rewards, promotions, and sometimes the removal of individuals. Incentives also include informal methods, such as the role model behavior of leaders and their daily reactions and feedback to employee conduct. In fact, depending on the details of the situation, the spontaneous reactions of the leaders might be even more influential than the formal incentive systems. High-performing organizations align their incentives (structured and unstructured) to ensure the best system + people = performance.

Bottom line: If you want a different organization, you have to change how you recognize and reward the people. All of these approaches have to be aligned and consistent with each other and the overall strategy and desired culture. The Align, Coach, Appreciate process is designed to help leaders provide feedback that improves follower performance, engagement, and commitment (Figure 9-1).

Figure 9-1 Align, Coach, Appreciate - System

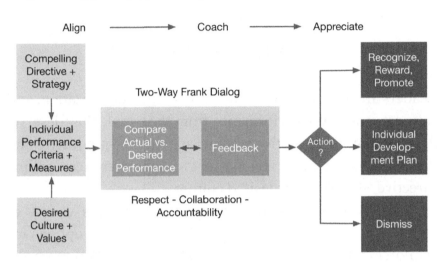

ALIGN

The first step is to align the criteria, measures, and methods used to evaluate employees with the organization's compelling directive, strategy, and desired culture. The alignment of the individual assessment is important because this is what will be used to incentivize the desired behaviors through the coaching and appreciation processes. It is difficult to overstate the importance of aligning the criteria and incentives that guide employee behavior with the overall strategy and desired culture. Yet it is common for leaders to say one thing, do another, and reward yet another.

This kind of confusion ends up with smart employees choosing for themselves the behavior that is in their own best interests. In short, actions speak louder than words, and incentives trump all else. Unfortunately, the misalignment of incentives might be the biggest issue preventing organizations from achieving the performance that they claim they desire.

Strategy

In addition to alignment, there is the need for a comprehensive system that includes all the key aspects of workforce performance. All too often the entire annual review process is based on the completion of a special project over and above the daily work responsibilities. This results in employees who do the minimum required toward their daily execution work and spend their time and energy on the projects that are evaluated as part of the review process. Why? That is where the money is.

However, strategy is more than new initiatives; it is the combination of daily execution AND improving daily execution. The performance assessment and feedback process needs to include a balance of each in order to create the results you really want today and tomorrow. Supporting the strategy is a culture of service.

Culture of Service

Reinforcing the desired behaviors requires that we clearly identify those desired behaviors. While work toward the mission, vision, and strategy is critical, doing that work in a way that is consistent with the desired culture and values of the organization is equally, if not more, important. All too often, we say we want a culture of teamwork, then reward and even promote individuals who help accomplish the strategy at the expense of their coworkers. In many organizations, it is individual performance that is rewarded regardless of team performance. When this occurs, everyone learns quickly what is really important.

I am reminded of the saying that culture reflects the worst behavior that is tolerated by leadership. If you want to accomplish the strategy and the desired culture, then both have to be aligned with the individual performance criteria, plan, and rewards.

Individual Assessment

Ultimately, we evaluate and reward individual performance to get the behavior we want. As one CEO put it, "You've got to make sure that the systems and tools are being used." The trick is to make sure that our criteria for individual evaluation is aligned with the strategy and culture. To do that, we have to identify the specific behaviors that will support our strategy and culture. Then we have to have the discipline and will to actually use that criteria to provide coaching, feedback, and incentives. While the workforce capabilities and the work are aligned in Chapter 5, the reinforcement and continuous development of the workforce is essential in daily practice. Alignment is critical, but without leadership, it is a waste of time.

COACH

The second step is to coach the workforce to help them meet the expectations identified in the individual performance criteria, culture, and strategy. Few things in the modern organization are hated more than the annual performance review process. All too often performance reviews resemble a pointless ritual: we do them because we are told to do them. And of course there are punishments if we don't comply. The result is often a go-through-the-motions, half-hearted attempt at filling a square so as not to get into trouble. Why? Many leaders do not see the value in the annual review process.

Three Issues with Performance Reviews

The first major issue is they are often too infrequent to be of much good. Humans learn best when the feedback is as immediate as possible following the action. Second, they are often encumbered with formality and legalistic activities that are not very useful for much of anything except documenting poor performance in case of litigation. Not that appropriate documentation isn't important, but managing to the lowest common denominator is not a recipe for a high-performing workforce. If you need to document all your employees' performance so you don't get sued when you make a decision, then you may have hired the wrong people and your time would be better spent improving your hiring process. Third, the feedback is often lacking any actionable information.

The main problem is you can't manage your way to a high-performing workforce. What is needed are leaders to inspire, coach, and appreciate their followers and lead them to high performance: leaders who correct poor performance and hold people accountable as needed. As many philosophers have noted, "There is no substitute for leadership."

Frequency and Formality

There are a few basic characteristics of individual performance reviews critical to successful transformation, including an individual scorecard that includes both running the organization and improving the organization. Two key design issues are the frequency and the formality. Annual performance reviews have come under fire for their lack of effectiveness at best and their demotivating impact at worst.

While some organizations are eliminating the individual performance review altogether, this may not be the best solution for your organization. Humans in general learn best when the feedback is sooner after the event. The sooner the better. One of the issues we face with trying to learn about how systems work is the delays that are often built in between the action and the result. When learning to walk, drive a car, and so on, the feedback is immediate. Turn the wheel and the car changes direction. Consequently, we learn to drive rather quickly. However, when there is a delay in the system we often do not recognize the connection between the action(s) and the result(s). This inhibits learning.

Designed for Management

So why would we build unnecessary delays into the workforce feedback system when we know that it is not effective for learning? The answer: it is easier for management and administration. The typical annual performance review is a tactical management tool designed by and for management with what appears to be little regard for their actual effectiveness in helping achieve the strategy.

An award winning organization CEO has a different approach. "Every employee can go on the intranet site and see where they are on every one of the goals that their entity level and system level . . . and see where they're performing against our goals and objectives." In order to provide immediate feedback, the design of the system has to be much easier to execute than most annual performance reviews, and leaders have to engage every day in aligning, coaching, and appreciating their followers.

APPRECIATE

William James proposed that "The deepest principle in human nature is the craving to be appreciated." Some leaders have told me that they limit the amount of praise they give, so the person doesn't get a "big head." I understand the concern. There is plenty of evidence to suggest that this is a real issue. However, the issue may be linked to the particular incentives and methods used to deliver them. The superficial, materialistic needs of the ego are not what James was referring to when he noted that appreciation was the "deepest" principle of human nature. People want their lives to have meaning and purpose. Leaders help inspire people with a compelling directive of the mission, vision, and values. But that needs to be reinforced with feedback, appreciation, and formal incentives.

The good news is showing your appreciation doesn't have to cost you any money, but it does require effort on your part. Choose your incentives wisely because when they are not aligned with the compelling directive, strategy, and culture, they can be counterproductive and result in reduced performance and turnover. High-performing organizations employ both leadership and systematic approaches to recognize, reward, and promote the desired behavior. As a last resort, leaders of high-performance organizations also make the tough decisions to let people go who are not able to develop and meet the expectations. This is unfortunate but sometimes necessary.

Recognition and Rewards

There is an old saying, "What gets measured gets done, and what gets rewarded gets repeated." Raises, bonuses, and promotions send a loud and clear message on what is really important. Consequently, the criteria and process for all three has to be aligned with the values and vision of the organization or you are wasting your time. If you promote someone who is not onboard, then your transformation is over. No one will believe you any longer. Once believability is gone, you no longer have the forces necessary to transform the organization.

High-performing organizations employ a wide variety of feedback, recognition, and reward tools and techniques. In one case, a CEO identified several practices including ". . . senior leader roundings, thank-you notes sent to employees' homes, standards of performance, behavior-based interviewing, peer interviewing, knowledgeable boards, employee communication sessions, team and empowerment ideas for excellence, reward and recognition. I mean, each one of these things is a major initiative in of itself."

However, extrinsic rewards and incentives often have a very short shelf life or impact, because they are focused on the short-term materialistic needs of the ego. It seems the ego can never be satisfied, and attempts to do so usually end in frustration and disappointment.

Problem with Extrinsic Incentives

People are often demotivated by the extrinsic incentives we provide, and in many instances would have been happier doing it for the simple enjoyment of the task (intrinsic motivation). Dr. Deming, in his system of profound knowledge, identified what he called the "phenomenon of overjustification" (Deming, 1994). But this isn't the only thing that is wrong with our current approaches to incentives.

Unfortunately, our current incentives often reduce performance — the opposite of the desired result. We have known this for a while, but management continues to ignore the empirical evidence. According to Dan Pink, the key to motivation for many contemporary jobs is not extrinsic financial rewards but rather intrinsic rewards and incentives around the concepts of autonomy, mastery, and purpose.

If you get nothing else from this passage, go watch Dan Pink's TED talk titled "The Puzzle of Motivation." Then use it to rethink the design of incentives in your organization.

Improve

Recognition and rewards are terrific when things are going well, but when an individual isn't meeting expectations, the individual performance review often results in an improvement or development plan. While all employees should be continuously developing their knowledge, skills, and abilities, sometimes there is a need for remedial training and coaching. When organizations change how they operate, employees often have to change to support the new process or strategy.

This transition can be more difficult for some employees than it is for others. Organizations undergoing major transformations provide support to help the workforce make the transition. Not every worker will get it the first time they are trained on the new method or direction. Patience and persistence are often required. However, for some organization transformations, a few people will never adapt and become successful in the new organization.

Remove

Unfortunately, organizations transformations sometimes result in a few casualties. If the transformation is large in scope and scale, then there are typically some members of the organization who do not get onboard and even some who actively undermine the changes. Much like promoting someone who is not in line with the direction of the organization, retaining someone who is not onboard or worse undermines the transformation — is also a message that you are not really serious. As one CEO noted, "So there was a very high expectation model ... we said we don't do it that way here, here is what you need to do and after the third time [not following the prescribed approach], we just said, look you don't need to be a leader here."

ALIGN AND INTEGRATE

Stakeholder Value - Knowledge of stakeholder segments, needs, and inter-relationships inform what behaviors we need to reinforce, as well as what types of reinforcement are effective for the workforce.

Compelling Directive - The compelling directive provides guidance on the type of behaviors that will support the mission of today and the vision of tomorrow. Included in the vision are the desired values which are translated into behaviors.

Focused Strategy - The behaviors and actions that support the strategic goals and objectives are reinforced. At the same time, behaviors and actions that do not support the strategic objectives are discouraged.

Enable, Empower, Engage - Behaviors that support enabling, empowering, and engaging the workforce are recognized and rewarded. Behaviors that discourage or detract from the enable, empowerment, and engagement are not tolerated and never inadvertently rewarded.

[Re]Design Systems - We reward system innovation and improvement. We don't punish failure: instead, we celebrate courage and creativity.

Comprehensive Scorecard - While we reinforce achievement of the desired results, we don't limit recognition to those things that can be measured quantitatively.

Organization Performance Review - Review results inform the recognition and rewards process. The results of the organization performance reviews identify those things that deserve recognition: both successes and prudent failures.

Learn and Improve - Consistent reinforcement of learning and improvement encourages engagement in learning and improvement activities. All too often, learning and improvement require going above and beyond one's normal duties. Reinforcement helps motivate engagement beyond the minimum required to do the job.

LEADER AS ORGANIZATION ARCHITECT

Leaders first must reinforce the desired behaviors by role-modeling those behaviors. Leaders of transformation personally participate in rewarding and recognizing those who demonstrate the desired behaviors.

While they might not enjoy it, effective leaders give tough feedback when needed. When leaders provide feedback, they do it with respect for the individual even when the feedback is negative or they have to let an employee go. Leaders at all levels communicate success stories widely throughout the organization. This helps identify and hold up those who consistently demonstrate the desired behaviors. In other words, the heroes of the organization: those who you want others to emulate.

Consistency is critical to overcoming skepticism and resistance to change. If you want collaboration, teamwork, systems thinking, and innovation, then you have to reward and reinforce those behaviors. More importantly, if you promote or reward someone who doesn't demonstrate those behaviors, all credibility will be lost. People are smart and will figure out quickly what you really want by YOUR behavior and your incentives.

REFLECTION QUESTIONS

Take a few minutes to reflect on your own organization and how you handle the systematic reinforcement of the desired behavior.

- Does your organization have explicit criteria for individual assessments that are aligned with your mission, vision, values, and strategy?

- Does your organization provide the necessary support for the workforce to be successful?

- Do you regularly recognize and reward the desired behaviors that are consistent with your mission, vision, values, and strategy?

- Do you promote ONLY those individuals who role-model the desired values?

Do you let individuals go who do not model the desired values?

Organization systems without people do not exist. While it is easy to design a system that will result in a bad performance and turnover, it is difficult to design a system that will result in engagement and high performance. With all systems, leadership is required to make them work. In this case, leadership must be willing and able to inspire, coach, and appreciate their people, while role-modeling that behavior every day.

Fortunately or unfortunately, leaders get the performance from the workforce that they deserve. It is up to the leader to decide what they really want and then do what is necessary.

10

LEARN AND IMPROVE

10

LEARN AND IMPROVE

INTRODUCTION

Results may not always reflect the performance that we had hoped for, but they always provide an opportunity for learning. If designed well, systems throughout the organization have learning loops built into the processes. While these learning loops take many forms, they are at their core, versions of the scientific method — or Plan, Do, Study, Act.

Unfortunately, many organizations and leaders are very good at "Plan, Do" — but they often do not take the time to study the results, learn from them, and adjust future actions based on those learnings. It doesn't have to be that way. We choose to learn or not. Creating and sustaining high performance requires a disciplined approach to learning from the past in order to create the desired future. Learning is built into several components of a well-designed leadership system.

Single and Double Loop Learning

While there are several types of learning that occur in organizations, there are two main types that occur when running and [re]designing organizations: single-loop and double-loop (Figure 10-1). Single-loop learning occurs when we execute the system, review the results, and adjust our techniques for implementing the system as it is currently designed. No system design changes are made in single-loop learning.

However, sometimes, no matter how hard we try to make it work, the system design is limiting the performance. Double-loop methods of learning include questioning the underlying design and assumptions in order to make changes to the design. In this last component of the leadership system, the focus is primarily on double-loop learning. First, the focus is on reflecting on the lessons learned during the organization performance reviews to inform revisions to the strategy and systems. Second, feedback from organization assessments are incorporated into the reflection process to add insights that are not included in the review of existing strategies and systems.

Figure 10-1 Single- and Double-Loop Learning

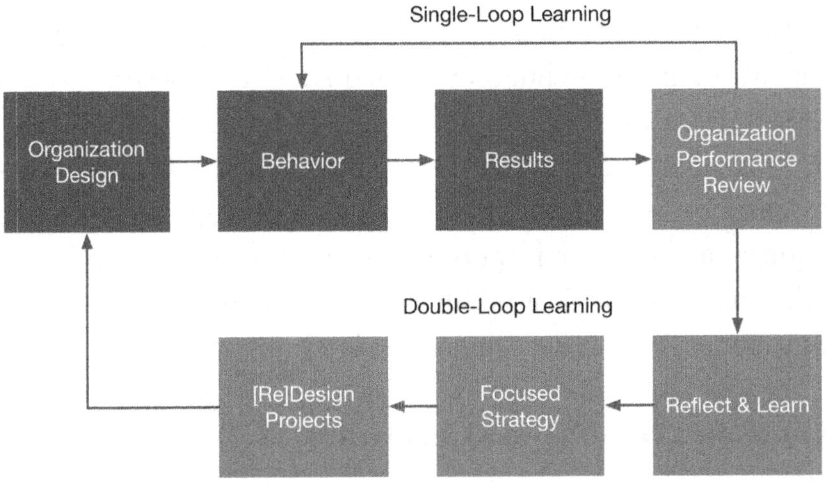

Learning from Success and Failure

Learning from success and failure is easier when we do not classify the results into these two categories. While organization performance reviews are typically conducted several times a year, every once in a while, it is time to sit down and take a deeper, more long-term look at both performance and progress. By classifying outcomes as either good or bad or success or failure, we are reducing rich data to simple categories. This results in a blunt instrument that covers up the detail needed to learn from the experience. Instead of passing judgment on the results with emotionally laden words, try simply thinking about the results as the outcome of an experiment to be studied.

When we say failure, people immediately try to cover up the details or pass the buck: anything to avoid being seen as a failure. When we say success, people sometimes get complacent and big-headed. Using less loaded language can help open the group member up to exploring the results and what occurred.

COMPLEX DYNAMIC SYSTEMS

It seems obvious that our organizations and the environments that they operate in are complex and dynamic. Yet there seems to be an insatiable appetite for simple answers. Unfortunately, many to most simplistic answers don't work. In the latter part of his life, Dr. W. Edwards Deming developed a system of profound knowledge that includes four components that help us understand organizations: systems, psychology, variation, and a theory of knowledge (Deming 1994). Deming's system of profound knowledge provides a framework for the richer, deeper understanding of the organization needed by the organization architect. The first component is an understanding of the organization as a system.

Organization as a System

Deming presented his notion of the organization as a system to Japanese executives in the 1950s when he introduced his "production system" (Deming, 1994). Since then, there have been a wide variety of perspectives on the organization system. These include Jay Forrester's work on dynamic systems, Michael

Porter's value chain, Russell Ackoff's work on organizations, plus excellence models such as the Malcolm Baldrige National Quality Award Criteria for Performance Excellence, which has been used by a wide variety of organizations to achieve and sustain high performance.

Bringing many of these ideas together and taking another step forward, Peter Senge focuses on the dynamic flow of interconnected activities and information in his 1990 book *The Fifth Discipline,* which also popularized "systems thinking." As Senge (1990) illustrates, it is one thing to think about individual exchanges between the interdependent components in a system and quite another to understand how the flows of energy and information play out over time in a dynamic system.

In dynamic organization systems, the distance between cause-and-effect is often separated in both time and space. The delay between action and result in organizations can be months or even years. The interaction and interdependence of the system components results in outcomes that show up in a system component far downstream of the initial action. Both the distance in time and space between action and result makes it difficult to transition from the endless reacting to symptoms and fighting fires toward identifying and fixing root causes and preventing fires. While systems approaches to organizations have helped leaders understand and create high performance, these systems are operated by a wide range of less predictable humans.

People

While systems are important to organizational performance, in organizations, systems are made of people. The people who occupy our organizations come in a wide variety of personalities, backgrounds, and motivations.

A lack of understanding of psychology all too often results in management practices and policies that do not work. Organizations are a combination of both systems and people, and one must understand both AND their interaction to truly understand organizations. Without an understanding of human behavior, we cannot understand organizations. And if we don't understand organizations, we cannot redesign them to perform better.

People come in infinite variety. When we combine them into groups, the permutations appear endless. This seems obvious, but when it comes to management practice and policy, we seem to act as if everyone is the same and are just like us. For example, we forget that people learn differently. The fact that people learn in different ways and at different speeds is obvious to even the least experienced teacher. Yet we continue to design training and education as if one size (combination of methods, sources, etc.) fits all. This variation combined with the variation in systems must be understood in order to understand the performance results and identify ways to improve those results.

System Variation

Organizational results vary because the people and processes vary. All too often managers fail to understand the normal variation inherent in organizational systems, and they react to the latest data point. When performance declines, managers often get involved and ask, "What you are going to do about the decline?"

However, if you react to the latest data points without

understanding the typical variation of the system, you may achieve only temporary improvement and you may ultimately cause even more variation. This is even more likely when there is a delay between the action and the results, as is often the case in organizational systems. Even when the overall trend is favorable, there are many data points along the way that are lower than the previous data point. When you understand the variation and overall trend in the system, you will know when to stay the course and when you need to make a change.

All too often, making changes in reaction to the latest data point ends up causing even more variation and poor performance: the opposite of your intent. Poor performance and variation are complex social phenomena that require a deep understanding of people and the systems and how they perform over time.

Theory of Knowledge

Unfortunately, all too often managers either do not have an explicit theory of knowledge or they unconsciously adopt the theory of knowledge that is embedded in their original education or discipline. For example, those with engineering or physical science backgrounds sometimes assume a positivist view of knowledge and the world, while those from the social sciences sometimes assume a constructivist view.

Organizations are composed of pieces, parts, and combinations that are sometimes predictable and relatively free of context (post-positivist) and other times they are highly context dependent and unpredictable (constructivist). Consequently, in management, we often adopt a pragmatic view that combines both of these views.

Leading and designing an organization requires both

critical and systems thinking with a clear understanding of the limits of our knowledge. Critical thinking is needed to identify and challenge the underlying assumptions in our thinking, recognize the importance of context, and imagine and explore alternatives. Systems thinking is needed to identify root causes, understand the distance and delays between cause and effect in organization systems, and develop solutions that will achieve the desired results. Ultimately, design thinking is needed to [re] design the organization to improve organization performance. In the end, it is all about learning and subsequent improvement.

FOUR APPROACHES TO LEARNING

The essence of sustainable excellence and a sustainable competitive advantage is to learn faster than your competitors. There are four learning methods common to organization that have achieved sustainable excellence (Figure 10-2).

The overall learning loop is the strategy development and deployment cycle. The needs of strategy drive the other

Figure 10-2 Four Approaches to Learning

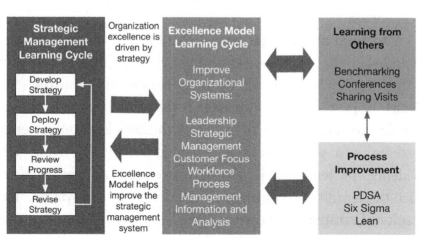

three learning methods and, in turn, strategy is supported by the contributions of the other three methods. Organization assessment is a separate and distinct learning loop where the organization plans the assessment, collects the data, studies and evaluates the data, and then proposes improvements to the systems. Continuous improvement process supports both the organization assessment and the strategy processes. And the projects for improvement often come from the strategy and assessment processes. Systematic methods used to learning from others support all three learning loops: strategy, assessment, and continuous improvement as well as the [re]design process.

Strategy Learning Loop

The strategy process is a large learning loop made of many smaller learning loops. Even the overall structure follows the scientific method of plan, do, study, act. The strategy development process includes a planning phase, a strategy deployment or "do" phase, a study the results during organization performance review phase, and an "act" phase where the plans are revised and adjusted based on the learning that took place during the study phase.

A focused strategy of goals and objectives is an untested hypothesis that predicts expected changes in performance if the strategy is deployed. Strategy deployment and the [Re] Design of products and processes is the test of that hypothesis. The design and redesign of the organization's key components, systems, and processes is a learning process by itself. The evidence of learning is the improvement of performance once the learning is captured in the design of the system. The results of strategy deployment (the test) are reviewed during the periodic organization performance review process (OPR). Finally, the results inform future changes to systems, strategy, scorecard, stakeholders, and the culture.

Organization Assessment

While organization transformation is primarily driven by strategy, an explicit excellence model increases the odds of a successful design or redesign. An enterprise systems model provides an explicit structure to assist in the alignment of the organization's stakeholders, strategy, systems, and scorecard. Whether you begin with an established excellence framework or develop your own, a model provides the top-level systems understanding that is required for designing the individual systems so that they contribute to the overall system success.

Many leaders who have successfully designed or [re]designed and transformed their organization used a model as a guide. Excellence models such as the Baldrige Criteria for Performance Excellence (MBNQA) or the European Foundation for Quality Management (EFQM) provide useful non-prescriptive frameworks to guide the design and redesign of custom organization systems. Organization-wide assessments go beyond the existing strategy and scorecard to provide a different perspective of the organization. Organization assessments using an excellence model force you to ask questions you never thought to ask.

Regardless of the model used, the Design Framework combined with a focus on system design provide the structure to design, develop, and deploy any new or redesigned initiative or system in the organization. Performance excellence criteria provide a map for developing the systems.

Design First then Assess

Applying for an excellence award before you understand your own systems is a waste of your time and examiner's time — it can also result in a loss of interest in the excellence journey itself. In addition, if you do not understand what the criteria questions mean, your answers are not going to make much sense. The result will be a feedback report from the examiners that says there is no evidence of a systematic approach: not very useful. You already knew that when you couldn't answer the questions. While the excellence award process is incredibly valuable, the real value from the feedback comes once you have solid systems in place that you can fully describe in the application.

Good news! There is an even better way to use the excellence models in the early stages of finding your way out of the weeds. An "align then design" approach to using the excellence model enables you to jump from where you are, to an aligned and integrated system. It allows you to skip the line of incremental cycles of improvement from no systematic approach to a basic approach to an aligned approach to an integrated approach in one step.

There is simply no reason to go through all the multiple cycles of feedback from an award process to get to a solid, systematic system that is aligned and integrated. Some of you may be thinking this is not possible. However, aligned and integrated doesn't mean it is fully developed and perfect: it will need further development and cycles of improvement and refinement. That is where the award process and feedback on the systems become incredibly valuable in reaching the goal of sustainable excellence. The point is to first design the best systems you can. After that, describing them in the award application will be easy, and the feedback from the examiners will be even more valuable and easy to understand.

Continuous Improvement Options

There are a variety of methods available to improve the systems in an organization, ranging from individual process improvement to overall organization system improvement. There is the long list of management fads promising to be THE answer to all that ails your organization.

Most of these actually worked if you did them correctly and stuck with it. In fact, I suspect most management fads failed due to leadership, not a problem with the method. There are several solid improvement methods that have been around for quite a while and they all work if you do it right. Continuous process improvement, Lean, and Six Sigma are used by many organizations to improve processes throughout their organizations. All of these methods are variations of the scientific method popularized by Walter Shewhart and W. Edwards Deming (Shewhart, 1931; Deming, 1986).

While each has a specific approach to the four steps of Plan, Do, Study, Act (PDSA), they all develop new methods, test those new methods, then learn and adjust as needed. All Baldrige Award recipients that I know of use one or more of these methods throughout their organization. Whatever particular path you choose, achieving and sustaining excellence requires continuous learning and improvement at all levels in the organization.

Learning from Others

Sometimes you just need a little inspiration from outside your own organization. Some have proposed that benchmarking leads to copying and thus following the competition. Indeed, it is a double-edged sword as I discuss in Chapter 6 "Inspiring Examples" section. However, I propose that if you are copying, you are doing it wrong.

Learning from others is not about copying: it is about inspiration and creative adaptation to create something new. The leaders of award-winning organizations all had a variety of ways to learn from others, from reading published case studies to attending conferences to actually visiting other high-performing organizations.

To get started, you don't have to leave your desk. The National Institute of Standards and Technology (NIST) in the United States has numerous examples of Baldrige Award recipients on their website. You can download for free the PDF versions of the award applications for the Baldrige Award recipients since 1999. The award application describes the organization systems for leadership, strategy, customer focus, human resources, operations, information and analysis, and the associated results. Go to: http://organizationdesignstudio. com/recreate-resources/ to get started learning. Also, make sure you study organizations outside of your industry. That is where some of the best ideas will come from.

ALIGN AND INTEGRATE

Results of learning inform the other eight components in the leadership system.

Stakeholder Value - The stakeholder segments and system of service provide a framework for organizing the learning and improvement activities. In addition, lessons learned help to refine the stakeholder segments and needs, as well as your understanding of the interrelationships between the stakeholders.

Compelling Directive - Learning and improvement support the mission today (what we do for stakeholders) and progress toward the vision of tomorrow. The vision includes all stakeholder segments.

Focused Strategy - Reflection and learning about the organization inform the strategy development process. Previous strategies are validated and lessons learned are used to develop refined or new strategies.

Enable, Empower, Engage - Learning and improvement is an integral part of enabling and empowering people to contribute toward the overall strategy and compelling directive. Engaging people in learning activities not only improves their capability but also encourages involvement in activities that contribute to the mission and vision.

[Re]Design Systems - The [re]design process itself is an iterative learning process that contributes to the overall understanding of the organization. What is learned from other learning and improvement processes also informs and enhances the [re]design process.

Comprehensive Scorecard - Learning and improvement processes rely on several inputs, including the results measured by the comprehensive scorecard.

Organization Performance Review - Results of the organization performance review process inform the reflection, learning, and improvement processes. The learning and improvement processes take the next step and go deeper into the analysis and learning required to make substantive changes to the organization.

Reinforce Behavior - Consistent reinforcement of learning and improvement encourages engagement in learning and improvement activities. All too often, learning and improvement require going above and beyond one's normal duties. Reinforcement helps motivate engagement beyond the minimum required to do the job.

LEADER AS ORGANIZATION ARCHITECT

Just like organization performance reviews, effective leaders of learning and improvement balance advocacy and inquiry to encourage collaboration during organizational learning activities. If you want innovation and risk taking, then don't kill the messenger.

Instead, create a safe environment where people are free to explore performance, regardless of where it falls on the scale of good to bad. Part of creating a safe environment includes respect for individuals and frank two-way communication to maximize learning during organization learning activities. Leaders demonstrate patience and tenacity when learning from the results of performance reviews and assessments. The effective leader is personally and tangibly involved in the organization learning activities and uses systems thinking to enhance the learning. Finally, effective leaders of sustainable excellence practice personal reflection and learning during organizational learning activities.

REFLECTION QUESTIONS

Successful leaders of transformation are never satisfied with the organization's performance and continually reflect on and learn from experience. They view every experience as an opportunity for learning.

> Do your leaders model the desired behaviors to facilitate dialogue and learning during organizational learning activities?

> Do you learn from each cycle of strategy development and deployment?

> Does your organization learn from organization assessments (e.g., Baldrige, EFQM, ISO)?

> Does your organization learn from continuous improvement projects (e.g., Six Sigma, Lean)?

> Does your organization learn from other organizations?

The design of the organization influences the behavior of the people inside and outside. The design is what people see and hear. What they think and feel about what they see and hear influences what they say and do (their behavior). Their behavior influences the results and overall organization performance. Developing the organization's systems, culture, and individual people requires that the organization learn not only from their successes but also from their failures. When we review organization performance we engage in two main types of learning: single-loop and double-loop. Single-loop learning occurs when the execution and management of the existing system is adjusted to achieve the best performance possible. Unfortunately, sometimes our best efforts fail to achieve the expected performance levels. Double-loop learning occurs when the underlying assumptions regarding the strategy and system design are examined and changed.

As others have noted, the only sustainable competitive advantage today is to learn faster than the competition. While we talk about organizations learning, it is the people in the organization that actually learn. And people learn when leaders set the example and learn too.

11

COLLABORATIVE LEADERSHIP

INTRODUCTION

Organization design is a collaborative process. No single individual knows enough to design an organization by themselves, although many try. Even if there were such an individual, involving others in the design helps reduce resistance to implementing the new design. In many ways, a collaborative leadership style is the art of leading transformation.

Figure 11-1 Collaborative Leadership Style - Components and Relationships

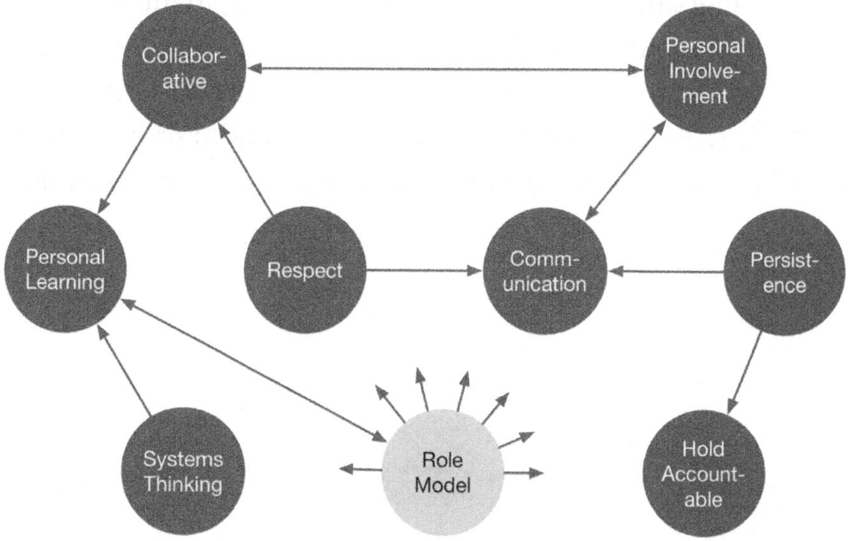

There are nine leader behaviors in the framework that support the system for leading design and transformation including (1) role model, (2) respect for people, (3) collaborative, (4) communication, (5) persistence, (6) hold accountable, (7) systems thinking, (8) personal involvement, and (9) personal learning (Figure 11-1). Together these nine behaviors form a collaborative leadership style that support the nine leadership activities in the leadership system (Chapters 2 through 10).

ROLE MODEL

We change the design of organizations expecting different behaviors. This change in behavior naturally requires individuals to change. To be credible, the leader as the chief organization architect (OA) must change first. Without credibility, the new design will fall flat and fail to change behavior.

There is an old saying in the military: "A leader is always on parade." The concept of a leader as a role model is probably in every leadership book and leadership development course on the planet — and for good reason. However, in this case, it takes on a slightly different connotation. The leader in this context has to learn and personally transform. As Gandhi proposed, you must become the change you want to see in the organization.

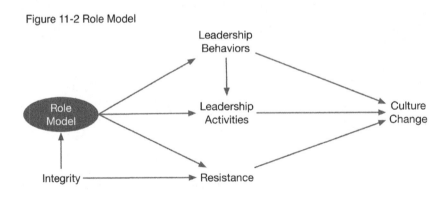

Figure 11-2 Role Model

Role model leadership is based on a foundation of the individual characteristic of integrity in the sense of a completely unbroken style. Leaders who set the example by role-modeling the behaviors and activities that are aligned with the desired culture help the organization's culture evolve (Figure 11-2). Leaders practicing what they preach also help reduce resistance to change. Effective leaders role-model the other eight behaviors that make up the leadership style of the organization architect, starting with respect for all people regardless of position or role.

Leadership Questions

Ask yourself how well you and your colleagues are role modeling the nine leadership activities.

1. Leaders set the example and lead the process of identifying stakeholders and their needs. Leaders set the example by building positive relationships with stakeholders.

2. What leaders say and do are aligned with and continuously reinforce the mission, vision, and values.

3. Leaders model the ability to prioritize and the discipline to follow through. Sometimes leaders demonstrate how to say "no," even to good ideas.

4. Leaders make sure everyone is enabled, empowered, and engaged in accomplishing the mission and vision.

5. Leaders set the example as the engaged and supportive "sponsors" of [re]design (strategy deployment) projects. They use their formal power to help the team navigate the organization network of what are often "self-serving silos."

6. Leaders develop and implement a comprehensive scorecard to measure the stakeholders, strategy, and systems.

7. Leaders personally role model balancing advocacy and inquiry during the organization review process discussions.

8. Leaders personally participate in recognizing and rewarding desired behavior and give tough feedback when necessary.

9. Leaders personally participate in organizational learning and improvement activities.

RESPECT FOR PEOPLE

Caring for and treating everyone fairly is an essential prerequisite for a culture of trust and teamwork. If you want people to collaborate and change, you have to treat them with respect. Successful organization architects treat people with respect and dignity regardless of position or status.

Respect creates an environment for engagement, collaboration, and innovation from top to bottom. The good news is respect is a natural and authentic behavior for leaders who are humble but confident. More on this in Chapter 13. When combined with a purpose to serve others and create value for multiple stakeholders, respect encourages collaboration, teamwork, and reduces resistance to change (Figure 11-3). All of which lead to a culture that is an employee focused "clan" as well as market- and customer-focused. More on this in Chapter 12.

Figure 11-3 Respect for People

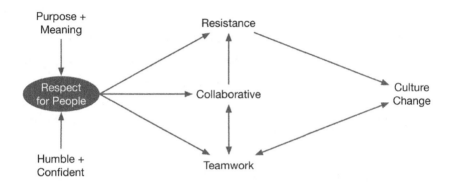

Leadership Questions

Ask yourself how well you and your colleagues are practicing respect as you perform the nine leadership activities.

1. Leaders show respect for all stakeholders, which helps build positive relationships with all stakeholder groups.

2. Leaders work toward a mission and vision that include building "win-win" relationships with multiple stakeholders.

3. Leaders set high but realistic goals that allow people to achieve high-quality work and avoid ethical dilemmas.

4. Leaders respect for individuals encourages continuous development, empowerment, and engagement.

5. Leaders encourage excellence by setting and enforcing high but reasonable expectations. At the same time, leaders treat everyone in the organization with respect, regardless of title or position.

6. To ensure leaders at all levels show respect for people, leaders include a measure of the level of respect for people in the annual employee survey.

7. Leaders always show respect for each individual, which encourages the frank, two-way dialogue necessary for open and honest organization performance reviews.

8. Leaders provide feedback with respect for the individual, including when letting employees go.

9. Leaders don't kill the messenger and create a safe environment where people are free to state their opinion, good or bad, as long as they do it respectfully.

COLLABORATIVE

Organization transformation is complex, and the challenges can be great. Creating sustainable excellence requires a collaborative leader and a team-based approach. As the CEO of IDEO, Tim Brown notes, "The increasing complexity of products, services, and experiences has replaced the myth of the lone creative genius with the reality of the enthusiastic interdisciplinary collaborator" (Brown, 2008, p. 87).

To [re]design the various aspects of the organization, leaders leverage the knowledge, creativity, and talents of a diverse team. To do this, successful organization architects are humble, respectful, and collaborative (Figure 11-4).

A prerequisite for collaboration seems to be a high level of humility combined with the confidence to advocate and lead. Leaders who successfully lead sustainable organization change don't think that having sole responsibility or credit is important.

Collaboration leads to reduced resistance to change, teamwork, and richer learning experiences. Collaboration also encourages teamwork and a culture of trust. As the old saying goes, "None of us are as smart as all of us."

Figure 11-4 Collaborative

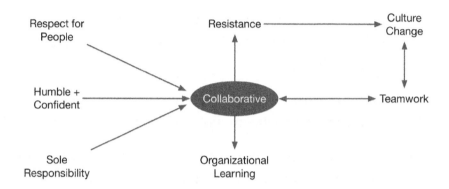

Leadership Questions

Ask yourself how well you and your colleagues are practicing collaboration while performing the nine leadership activities.

1. Leaders involve stakeholders (or their input) in setting the direction and evaluating progress.

2. Leaders involve key stakeholders (or their input) in the development of the mission, vision, and values of the organization.

3. Leaders facilitate a strategy process that is inclusive and collaborative.

4. Leaders involve and engage people in the collaborative planning, execution and improvement of all work.

5. Leaders involve key stakeholders throughout the organization in the [re]design projects and transformation required to achieve the mission and vision.

6. Leaders involve stakeholders (or their input) in developing the key performance measures that make up the comprehensive scorecard.

7. Leaders conduct organization performance reviews as a collaborative cross- functional group, which results in a rich team dialogue.

8. Leaders reward collaboration and avoid rewarding (e.g., promoting) those who are not collaborative team players.

9. Leaders balance advocacy and inquiry to encourage collaboration during organizational learning activities.

COMMUNICATION

Design is communication. The design of an organization is manifested in information artifacts that communicate the systems, strategy, methods, and values. Part of organization design and transformation is frequent communication using both formal and informal media and methods to convey the need for change as well as the approach to change. Frank two-way dialogue with stakeholders is a critical skill of organization architect leaders.

Figure 11-5 Communication

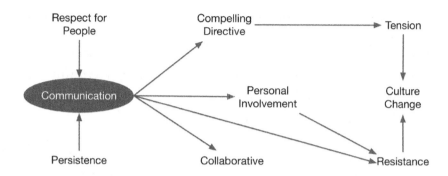

Communication that is consistent and respectful encourages collaboration, which helps reduce resistance to change (Figure 11-5). Personal involvement in frank, two-way communication with stakeholders improves the design and facilitates the necessary culture change. It also provides a medium for feedback that is often only available through face-to-face dialogue. In addition, consistent and persistent communication of the compelling directive helps create positive tension and culture change. However, "Actions speak louder than words" is a cliché for a reason. See role model discussion.

Leadership Questions

Ask yourself how well you and your colleagues are practicing communication while performing the nine leadership activities.

1. Leaders communicate (two-way dialogue) with stakeholders to gather information and communicate the direction and progress of the organization.

2. Leaders regularly and effectively communicate the com-

pelling directive (mission, vision, values) to the multiple stakeholders.

3. Leaders communicate the strategic goals and clear expectations to the multiple stakeholders.

4. Leaders regularly engage in frank two-way communication with employees to enable, empower, and engage them toward the mission and vision.

5. Frank two-way communication at all levels addresses critical issues before they become difficult problems in the [re]design projects.

6. Leaders communicate the scorecard measures, how they were selected, what they mean, and how they will be used.

7. Leaders balance inquiry and advocacy to create an environment that encourages open and frank two-way communication and dialogue during the organization performance reviews.

8. Leaders communicate and celebrate success stories AND innovative failures widely throughout the organization to reinforce the desired behaviors.

9. Leaders create the environment for frank, two-way communication to maximize learning during organization learning activities.

PERSISTENT

Most employees have seen a wide variety of change initiatives come and go. Leaders often have difficulty following through with the actual change. Why? One reason might be that developing strategies is a lot more fun than the hard work of actually implementing the strategy and running the organization. Nicolò Machiavelli might have summed it up best with his now famous quote from *The Prince*.

> *"It must be considered that there is nothing more difficult to carry out nor more doubtful of success nor more dangerous to handle than to initiate a new order of things; for the reformer has enemies in all those who profit by the old order, and only lukewarm defenders in all those who would profit by the new order; this lukewarmness arising partly from the incredulity of mankind who does not truly believe in anything new until they actually have experience of it."*

Figure 11-6 Persistent

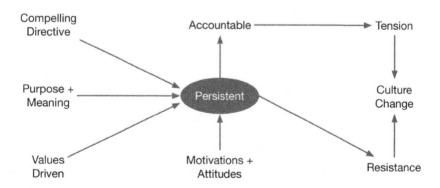

Not surprisingly, successful organization architects are tenacious and persistent. Even when faced with resistance they never blink — even if they secretly have doubts about the change. While open to honest assessment and discussion, successful leaders of transformation continuously reinforce the mission, vision, values, and strategy of the organization (Figure 11-6). Consistency of message and actions helps reduce resistance to change. In addition, holding people accountable helps increase the tension to overcome the status quo. The reduced resistance and increased tension work together to help transform the organization and culture.

Leading change is an endurance test that requires a daily dose or energy. Or, as one CEO put it, "You have to go in and blow up the balloon every day."

Leadership Questions

Ask yourself how well you and your colleagues are demonstrating persistence while performing the nine leadership activities.

1. Leaders are persistent when it comes to building relationships with and creating value for multiple stakeholders regardless of the many challenges.

2. Leaders are persistent in communicating and reinforcing the mission, vision, and values.

3. Leaders consistently focus on strategic goals and objectives until they are complete.

4. Leaders constantly reinforce employee empowerment and engagement through their behaviors, communications, and actions.

5. Leaders require regular updates on the status of initiatives and operational results.

6. Leaders push for the continuous development and refine-

ment of the enterprise scorecard to support deeper system understanding and fact-based management.

7. Leaders have the tenacity and patience to develop a "team" culture with a systems perspective during organization performance reviews.

8. Leaders provide frequent and consistent reinforcement of the desired change to overcome resistance.

9. Leaders have the patience and tenacity to learn from and act on the results of changes made during organizational learning activities.

HOLD ACCOUNTABLE

Successful organizational transformation requires leaders follow through and hold people accountable. Many organizations develop compelling visions and strategies, but skip the steps required to make the vision a reality. Once the vision and strategy are set, successful leaders follow through and hold people accountable for the necessary changes in behavior and system design. Most importantly, holding people accountable helps maintain the tension necessary for successful organization transformation and culture change (Figure 11-7).

While the Align, Coach, Appreciate approach in Chapter 9 is the primary method to help people make the necessary change, when it doesn't work leaders sometimes have to remove employees. While in many cases some of these employees voluntarily leave on their own, sometimes they have to be forced to leave. Tolerance of behaviors and actions that are not consistent with the organization's chosen direction will undermine the transformation. If someone can succeed in

Figure 11-7 Hold Accountable

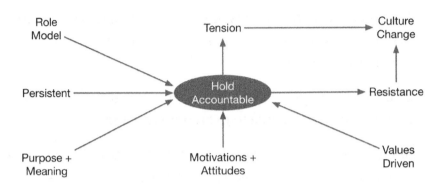

the organization without supporting the transformation, the transformation is doomed.

Leadership Questions

Ask yourself how well you and your colleagues are doing holding people accountable while performing the nine leadership activities.

1. Leaders turn "forced" (often adversarial) accountability to stakeholders into proactive win-win relationships and a positive force for change.

2. Leaders hold people accountable for progress toward the mission and vision.

3. Leaders hold people accountable for staying focused and achieving the strategic goals.

4. Leaders hold people accountable for their personal development and improvement of the organization.

5. Leaders hold people accountable for developing, implementing, and managing [re]design projects.

6. Leaders hold people accountable for fact-based management and decision-making.

7. Leaders consistently hold the team accountable for short- and long-term organization performance.

8. Leaders hold people accountable for the desired change including removing employees if necessary.

9. Leaders hold people accountable for continuous improvement of organization performance as an integral part of their job.

SYSTEMS THINKING

Achieving and sustaining high performance requires systems thinking to identify the leverage points that will have the greatest impact on overall organization performance for the least amount of effort and expense. Not only are successful leaders skilled at systems thinking, but they are also strongly motivated to work with systems and processes (Figure 11-8). Successful leaders of change are systems thinkers and able to connect the dots to create an aligned and congruent organization.

Systems thinking in organizations often requires collaboration across functional boundaries. It is rare for a single individual in an organization to fully understand multiple functional areas. Consequently, systems thinking in organizations is usually a collaborative exercise. The benefit of this collaboration is increased teamwork and learning (both individual and organizational).

Systems thinkers do not view the world as a zero-sum game. Instead, they enable, empower, and engage people to create high-quality products and services that create satisfied customers who come back (repeat business) and bring their friends (referral business). Naturally, this leads to happy investors. A deep understanding of the organization system enables changes that improve the overall performance of the organization.

Figure 11-8 Systems Thinking

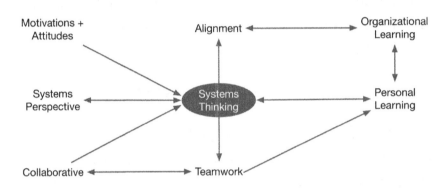

Leadership Questions

Ask yourself how well you and your colleagues are practicing systems thinking while performing the nine leadership activities.

1. Leaders avoid taking from one stakeholder to serve another and instead develop win-win situations that create value for all the stakeholders.

2. Leaders have developed a mission and vision that focus on the sustainable success of the entire organization system.

3. Leaders develop strategic goals that focus on leverage points in the system to create the desired results.

4. Leaders understand the connections between employee capability and engagement and enterprise performance.

5. Leaders sponsor and support the development and deployment of cross-functional [re]design initiatives.

6. Leaders develop scorecards that measure the system components to support the analysis of the overall system.

7. Leaders analyze the enterprise system relationships between the measures to gain insights and identify leverage points to improve performance.

8. Leaders reward systems thinking and reject solutions that are narrowly based on individual functions.

9. Leaders use systems thinking to enhance individual and organizational learning activities.

PERSONAL INVOLVEMENT

"Leadership is a contact sport" (Goldsmith and Morgan, 2005). Organization [re]design and transformation requires the personal involvement of leaders. You can't delegate the overall design and integration of the organization system. As one CEO noted, "You can't lead transformation from behind your desk." Even self-proclaimed introvert leaders have a systematic method to ensure they press the flesh and make the rounds.

Organization architect leaders regularly spend time communicating with stakeholders (Figure 11-9). Some have developed personal scorecards that depict where they spend their time. They set goals for the amount of time spent with key stakeholders from employee conversations to listening to the customer care line. For some leadership teams, the public comparison of their scorecards created a culture of good-natured competition. Personal involvement sets the example for other leaders and helps reduce resistance to change. Successful leaders make sure that people have what they need to do their job and execute the action plans.

Figure 11-9 Personal Involvement

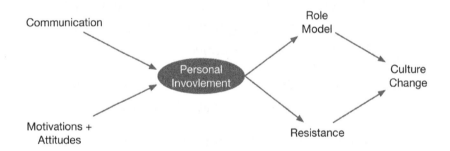

Leadership Questions

Ask yourself how you and your colleagues are personally involved in the nine leadership activities.

1. Leaders personally spend time with stakeholders, building relationships and developing a deeper understanding of their needs.

2. Leaders engage people at all levels in the discussion and translation of the mission and vision.

3. Leaders help people stay focused and avoid shooting from the hip when engaging with people throughout the organization.

4. Leaders regularly make the rounds with employees to check on key aspects related to employee engagement.

5. Leaders participate in [re]design activities and facilitate meetings when necessary to role model the way.

6. Leaders are personally involved in the development and improvement of the comprehensive scorecard.

7. Leaders are personally involved in the organization review process dialogue, findings, and follow-up.

8. Leaders are personally involved in recognition and rewards to reinforce the desired behavior.

9. Leaders are personally and tangibly involved in the organization learning activities.

PERSONAL LEARNING

Successful leaders of transformation are never satisfied with themselves or their organization. The successful leader of change becomes the change they want to see, and they do this through reflection and learning from education and experience. Leading transformation requires leaders at all levels reflect on the past and use experience to make decisions and develop strategies for achieving competitive advantage. As one follower put it when asked why they were not making the changes necessary for the transformation they said, "I will change when I see the CEO change."

Figure 11-10 Personal Learning

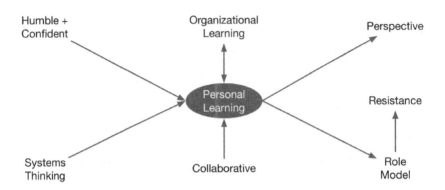

While success is often fun to learn from, it is just as important to learn from failures. Learning from success and failure is key to achieving sustainable high performance. Humility, systems thinking, and collaboration all enhance personal learning (Figure 11-10). It is difficult to learn when you think you know it all. The ego might be the biggest barrier to learning: humility reduces that barrier and enhances learning. Systems thinking enhances learning beyond simple facts and knowledge of individual components to understanding how the components are related and interact. This kind of learning informs changing the design of systems to obtain different results. Finally, collaboration enhances the learning process by adding additional perspectives to the discussion. Personal learning is essential for improvement and sets the example for everyone in the organization.

Leadership Questions

Ask yourself how well you and your colleagues are practicing personal learning while performing the nine leadership activities.

1. Leaders are continuously learning from stakeholders and developing new and innovative ways to meet their needs.

2. Leaders regularly reflect on and revise the compelling directive that helps give meaning and purpose to people.

3. Leaders regularly reflect on their behavior to ensure they stay focused on the key objectives.

4. Leaders model personal learning and continuous development.

5. Leaders listen, reflect, and learn from their experiences and personal involvement with [re]design projects.

6. Leaders measure personal learning and improvement at all levels.

7. Leaders are reflective and take the time to learn from the organization performance review process.

8. Leaders recognize and reward personal and organizational learning and development.

9. Leaders practice personal reflection and learning during our organizational learning activities.

REFLECTION QUESTIONS

1. Take a moment to summarize your overall performance based on the nine behaviors.

Based on the nine behaviors, what are your strengths?

Which of the nine behaviors do you demonstrate as a leader?

Which of the nine behaviors do you need to improve?

2. Now take a moment to assess your colleagues as a group of leaders.

> Based on the nine behavior, what are your colleagues' strengths?

> As a group, which of the nine behaviors does your leader colleagues demonstrate consistently?

> As a group, which of the nine behaviors does your leader colleagues need to improve?

The nine behaviors of collaborative leadership combined with the leadership system activities (Chapters 2 through 10) make up the core of the leadership approach to organization [re]design and transformation. On the surface, it seems like a lot to remember.

The good news is the nine leadership activities (Chapters 2 through 10) are systematic approaches that are made explicit and described in formal documents; they do not need to be remembered. The nine leadership behaviors (Chapter 11) can be learned to the point that they become habit. Both the leadership system and collaborative style influence the culture of the organization.

12

CULTURE OF SERVICE

INTRODUCTION

While the design of the leadership and management systems is the first signal of leadership intent, the ultimate goal is the overall organizational culture change. Culture is the glue that holds the organization together and makes it come alive. For our purposes, culture can be defined as "the collective programming of the mind which distinguishes the members" of the organization from other organizations (Hofstede, et al. 2010). It is learned and includes the patterns of thinking, feeling, and behaving in the context of the organization.

At the core of culture are the values of the organization which are manifested in the rituals, heroes, and symbols of the organization (Hofstede, et al. 2010). Sustaining excellence requires the new systems, processes, and practices become second nature and embedded in patterns of thinking and behavior. To achieve sustainable excellence, we need a culture of service to one another and all our stakeholders.

While internally oriented family or clan cultures can become self-serving and internally focused, it doesn't have to be that way. Organizations that have achieved performance excellence were able to focus on the external customers and market AND the workforce at the same time. They did it by valuing employees who trust each other and work together to create excellent products, services, and experience for customers. High-performing organizations are values-driven. Values drive decisions, behaviors, and priorities at all levels of the organization.

Values-driven

The Competing Values Framework proposes that the values of a CLAN culture (great for people) and a MARKET culture (great for customers) are "competing values" (Cameron and Quinn, 1999). Consequently, some have proposed that you have to choose between "competing values" — you can either have a great place to be an employee OR you can have a great place to be a customer, but not both.

However, Kim Cameron and Robert Quinn found that clan and market cultures are complementary and not competing for organizations that use Total Quality Management (TQM) (Cameron and Quinn, 1999). We found the same thing in our CEO study for organizations pursuing Baldrige-based Performance Excellence (Latham, 2013b). More good news: when leaders take a systems approach to designing the organization systems and culture, then employees-focused cultures and customer-focused cultures are complementary, making win-win arrangements possible (Figure 12-1).

Figure 12-1 Culture of Service

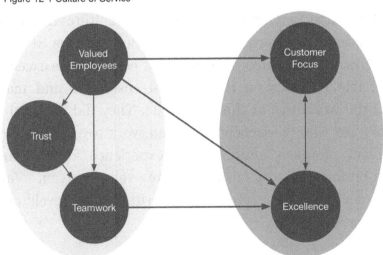

High performance is dependent on high levels of customer satisfaction and thus "customer-driven" is a key cultural value. As one CEO put it, ". . . it is not about the performance excellence model. It's about the culture of patient satisfaction still at the 99% percentile and employee satisfaction still at the 99% percentile." Great customer experiences are the result of highly capable and motivated employees, systematic approaches that help your employees create memorable experiences for customers, and the overall culture and climate of the organization. Creating great customer experiences is the key to developing loyal customers who come back for more and bring their friends and family with them.

Customers are the objective of the market-oriented culture. If you take a systems perspective, then a clan culture focused on the people can result in customer experiences that result in repeat and referral business. In other words, you can have both, as many organizations have demonstrated. Organizations that were successful in achieving sustainable excellence had five core values in common: valued employees, trust, teamwork, excellence, and customer focus.

Valued Employees

While our mission might be to serve an external market or customer, we must start building the culture with the workforce. Unless the individual is valued, there is no hope of engaging them in a higher purpose. A culture that is respectful of and values employees is a key cultural characteristic of a high-performance culture (Figure 12-2). As one CEO put it, "The thing that did change was I began to understand really how important everything I said and did was to the culture of the organization.

And I learned that not only do you have to be caring, you have to be demonstrably caring."

Figure 12-2 Valued Employees

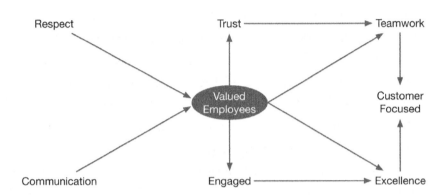

Some have suggested that leaders need to adjust their style for different types and generations of followers. However, there is evidence that if a leader adopts a servant leadership style, one size might fit all (Zimmerer and Latham, 2014). A servant leader approach sets the example for a workforce that is focused on serving each other as internal customers and the external customers. In other words, valued employees create satisfied customers. As one healthcare CEO said, "I expect employees to provide the best patient service, and it isn't fair if I don't first meet the employees' needs." Valued employees are the foundation for trust and teamwork.

Trust

With trust, teamwork is possible. Without trust, nothing is possible. The combination of respect and trust creates an environment that encourages collaboration and teamwork which leads to excellence and customer satisfaction (Figure 12-3). The changes in the organization that are needed to achieve high performance are designed and developed through collaboration, giving the participants a sense of ownership in the strategies and solutions.

Figure 12-3 Trust

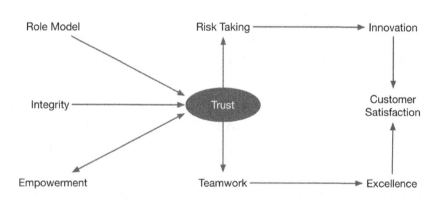

This sense of ownership, combined with trust among the team members, creates an environment for excellence in execution and customer service. Consequently, a leadership style of respect is essential to trust, teamwork, and collaboration. Innovation to achieve excellence requires risk and learning from BOTH failure and success. If the organization has created a culture of fear and mistrust, they need to look at the leadership styles that are prevalent in the organization. Failure does not inherently create fear. It is poor leadership that creates fear by the way they handle failure. One way they do this is by focusing on the primary causes of failure, which is the organization systems, not the people. Ultimately, it is teamwork that creates the products, services, and experience for the customers.

Teamwork

Cross-functional teamwork and knowledge-sharing are common to high-performing organizations. As one CEO described it, "Teamwork in the sense of agreeing to the vital few through the strategic planning goal deployment process and working together . . . In the past, we still acted functionally, so we had to move from a functional organization to a more of a team-based, process-driven organization." Teamwork characterized by cooperation, collaboration, and knowledge-sharing enhances innovation, excellence, and ultimately customer satisfaction (Figure 12-4).

In team sports, individual talent is critical, but only when it works as a team. According to Isiah Thomas, in Bill Simmons' *The Book of Basketball: The NBA According to the Sports Guy*, "The secret of basketball is that it's not about basketball." It is about playing a complementary role that fills a void in the team in a way that helps your teammates play better than if you were not on the team.

Figure 12-4 Teamwork

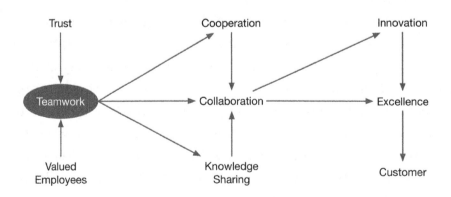

The corollary: The secret of business is that it isn't about business. It is about individual effort and engagement that makes the other members perform better than they would if you weren't on the team. In short, it takes a team of talented people who trust each other to produce excellence for customers.

Excellence

Excellence in everything we do is the objective of the high-performing organization. Unfortunately, the term "excellence" has become overused and somewhat meaningless. However, for our purposes, excellence is a central concept of exceeding expectations for multiple stakeholders. Integral to a culture of excellence is continuous learning and improvement. Quality, innovation, and continuous learning and improvement are essential for a high-performing culture.

Excellence is the opposite of "good enough." Excellence is enhanced by teamwork, learning, innovation, and a customer focus (Figure 12-5). In addition, an excellence-focused strategy supported by [re]design projects also increases customer satisfaction.

Figure 12-5 Excellence

As one CEO described it, "We couldn't get the production line schedule to stabilize to deliver on time because of the manufacturing guys were schedule-driven and not quality-driven. And he said, stop the line, don't move the product, and these manufacturing guys looked at us like, . . . he's lost it." The organization architect leader is responsible for creating an environment for excellence and innovation. Excellence and innovation are inextricably linked. Sustainable excellence is dependent on continuous innovation of all types including management innovation. Consequently, a culture of curiosity and creativity underpins constant innovation and excellence. While the focus of excellence is on all the stakeholders, it is the basis of exceptional customer experiences.

Customer Focus

Customer focus combined with excellence and innovation is the objective of the market-oriented culture (Figure 12-6). High performance for the organization and multiple stakeholders is dependent on high levels of customer satisfaction and thus "customer-focus" is a key cultural value. As discussed in Chapter 2, customers are not just applicable to profit-seeking organizations. Non-profits also have customers — the primary beneficiaries of their products and services (e.g., hungry children). Government organizations also have customers of their particular services (e.g., residents of safe neighborhoods). Positive customer experience is the combination of highly capable and motivated employees, systematic approaches that help employees create memorable experiences for customers, and the overall culture and climate of the organization. Creating great customer experiences is the key to developing loyal

Figure 12-6 Customer Focus

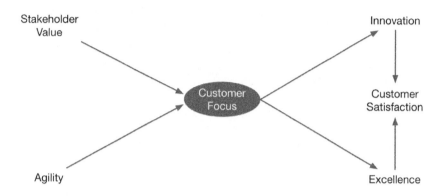

customers who come back for more and bring their friends and family with them. The goal of culture is for the values to become habits.

DEVELOPING CULTURE

Some have proposed that culture cannot be designed directly, and instead is an outcome of the other components of organization design including strategy and systems. While this is true, the tangible manifestations of culture can be designed as part of organization design. The values of the organization are manifested in the rituals, heroes, and symbols, all of which can be purposefully designed as part of the organization design. All too often, cultures emerge from an unplanned, extemporaneous collection of events and behaviors that occur over time. These events, behaviors, and beliefs become habits embedded in the culture. While this might be common, it doesn't have to be this way. Culture can be designed and influenced though the tangible components of culture (Figure 12-7).

Figure 12-7 Components of Culture

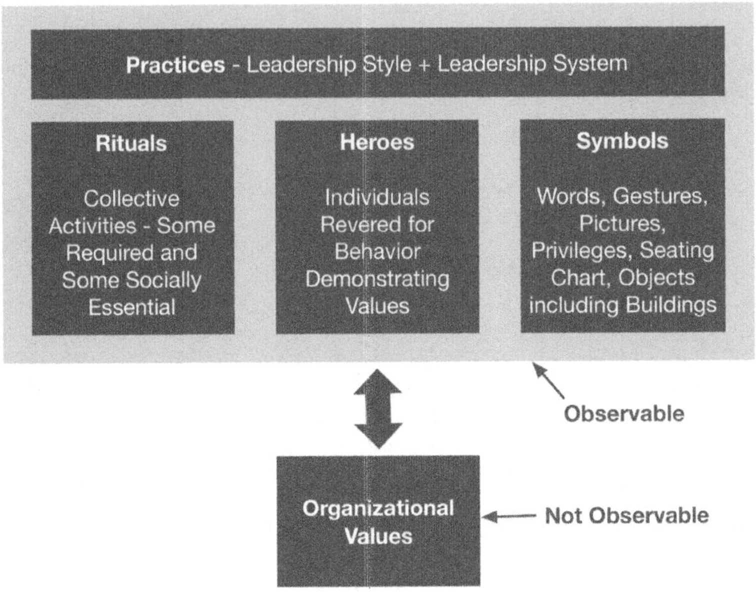

We can systematically redesign the rituals, heroes, and symbols to reflect the values that we desire in the organization and thus influence the patterns of thought and behavior.

Rituals, Heroes, Symbols

The rituals, heroes, and symbols of an organization are tangible and can be [re]designed to reflect the desired values. The word ritual is often associated with religion, but it can be any sequence of steps (often symbolic) taken that have a meaning such as a rite of passage (e.g., a wedding ceremony).

Organizations have many rituals, from annual strategy retreats to award ceremonies and celebrations such as retirement parties. These rituals reflect the values of the organization and also reinforce those values. The rituals are often designed to celebrate the top performers or heroes of the organization. As Mom used to say, "Choose your friends wisely." The corollary for the organization is choose your heroes wisely. Your choices reflect your values. You might say you value teamwork, but if your heroes (those you celebrate and promote) are not team players then no one will believe you.

Finally, symbols are everywhere from the reserved parking places to the corner offices to those who get to fly first class. Symbols are powerful and also reflect what you truly value. The good news, all these things were created by humans and can be recreated by you to influence the culture to be what you want it to be. In addition to informal rituals, the systems, processes, and policies also reflect your values and send messages about what is important.

Systems Change

A common theme that continues to emerge from our experience and research on leading the organization [re]design is the notion of changing the system to change the thinking and behavior of the organization members. The power of changing the system vs. focusing on fixing people is not a new idea. W. Edwards Deming, Russell Ackoff, and others have suggested that the system is the main cause of behavior in organizations and that management is the only group that can change the system.

Changing the system influences the culture. For example, the compelling directive (mission and vision) influences the culture of customer focus. The design of the enable, empower, engage people systems influences the culture of valued employees. At the same time, culture informs the design of systems to fit the values. For example, the culture of excellence drives the inclusion of continuous learning and improvement loops in systems throughout the organization.

To change actions requires leaders redesign the systems. Unfortunately, organizations often approach system change with an engineering mindset vs. a human stakeholder mindset and then wonder why their new system didn't achieve the desired results. Organization systems are, at their core, human systems. Consequently, creating sustainable organization change requires a social systems thinking approach.

Leadership Style

Individual behavior and habits also influence the culture. For example, leadership behaviors of collaborative and system thinking encourage teamwork — in particular, cross-functional teamwork. Role model behavior encourages trust, which influences teamwork. At the same time, culture influences leader behavior change as people adapt to new values. For example, a culture of trust encourages collaboration and personal learning. Also, an employee-focused culture encourages respect for people.

Culture change requires individual change. Sustainable change requires that the individuals change and grow, which is often the hardest part of the change process. At the core of this change is a typical learning process where the gray matter gets grayer and the grooves get deeper. For some people this process can be unpleasant and is often resisted, but it is necessary, and it all starts at the top. If the leadership team is not learning, the organization design process will not make much difference.

The Habit

The longer the new system is in place, the greater the chance the new behaviors and methods will become habits and result in enduring transformation of the organization. Organizations have a memory, and if reinforcement isn't consistently applied, people will revert to the old way of doing business. This lack of follow-through is all too common as leaders often are off developing the next new idea before the last change is fully embedded.

If leaders are persistent and continue to reinforce this change, it will eventually result in sustainable culture change. Leaders need enough self-control to see the current change through before they move on to another initiative. In other words, sustainable transformation requires follow-through and tenacity.

REFLECTION QUESTIONS

Reflect on the following questions based on your experience in your organization.

Do the members of your organization value each other regardless of position in the organization?

Do the members of your organization trust each other?

Do the members of your organization work as a team and cooperate to accomplish the mission of the organization?

Do the members of your organization have high product and service standards and consistently meet those standards?

Do the members of your organization continuously learn and improve?

Are the members of your organization focused on creating products and services that delight the customers?

Aristotle proposed that "Quality is not an act. It is a habit." Culture change is not a quick fix. It takes time, tenacity, and a conscious combination of system [re]design and leadership. While all the leaders in our study wanted the culture to change quickly, as one CEO put it, "While you may have to put the 'rudder over hard,' the ship doesn't turn quickly. It takes time for culture change and you have to take the group along with you." While everything you need to lead system and culture change can be learned, it is easier if you have a few enabling characteristics, attitudes, and motivations.

13

THE INDIVIDUAL LEADER

INTRODUCTION

Sustainable organization transformation includes systems change, culture change, and individual change. Implementing the leadership style and system consistently and maintaining enough persistence to change the culture requires that the behaviors and activities be authentic. Leadership activities (system) and behaviors (style) are observable to the followers. However, behind these activities and behaviors are hidden dimensions including personality, ego, perspective, attitudes, and motivations. Successful leaders of transformation to sustainable excellence have five characteristics in common that increase the odds of achieving and sustaining high performance.

Purpose and Meaning - The leaders of high performance have a deep personal meaning and a sense of purpose focused on serving people.

Humble but Confident - Successful leaders of organization design and transformation are humble but confident.

Integrity - Leaders of transformation have a high degree of integrity that increases their credibility as a role model.

Systems Perspective - Organization architects have an uncommon world view. They view the world as a dynamic interrelated system vs. a static zero-sum game.

Attitudes and Motivations - Successful leader attitudes and motives were consistent with the behaviors and activities required by the tasks of design and transformation.

If the individual characteristics below the surface are not consistent with the behaviors and activities then the collaborative leadership style and activities is an unsustainable facade. The good news is these characteristics are changeable.

PURPOSE & MEANING

Leaders of high performance have a deep sense of purpose and find meaning in their work serving others (Figure 13-1). They communicate the mission and vision to help provide meaning for the entire workforce. When asked what they were most proud of as the leader of a successful organization transformation to sustainable excellence, the CEOs in our study shared anecdotes that included employees doing extraordinary things that contributed to the success of the team and customers. The stories of healthcare (patients) and education (students) were particularly poignant. These CEOs got their "kicks" by making it possible for others to succeed.

Figure 13-1 Purpose and Meaning

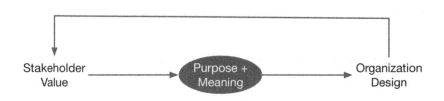

As a CEO of a healthcare organization noted, "The most satisfying thing to me is that our people are more engaged and happier and feel proud of what they do and feel proud of what they accomplished, and that they make a difference for the people they're treating." The leader's inner life/mindfulness influences their level of hope/faith and altruistic love which influences the followers' sense of calling and feeling of membership (Fry, Latham, Clinebell, and Krahnke, 2016). In other words, a deep sense of purpose to serve others enhances the leader's ability to lead a transformation to create systems and a culture that serves multiple stakeholders. Ultimately, this may be the secret of business. People with purpose are engaged and are happy because they are serving a greater cause than themselves.

HUMBLE AND CONFIDENT

Successful organization architect leaders occupy an intermediate position on the continuum between extreme humility and arrogance. This humble but confident characteristic enhances their collaboration because they don't think they know everything, but at the same time, they advocate for their ideas. They balance advocacy and inquiry, which is a key to effective dialogue and design. They are excellent listeners, explore many perspectives, are empathetic, and are not motivated by personal recognition for their achievements.

Leaders of sustainable excellence are motivated to serve and make the overall organization successful. They are motivated to help enable the accomplishments of their team to better serve the customers. The low need for personal recognition and sole responsibility combined with a collaborative leadership style, and a systems thinking approach, create an environment for synergistic problem solving and creative designs and strategies for sustaining excellence and innovation. These approaches to leadership eventually lead to organizational culture change and the embedding of teamwork throughout the organization culture.

The most important benefit of leader humility is they can face the truth of the current organization design and performance. Unless the leaders are honest and objective about the organization there is no hope for a new design. But to be effective, the leader has to be authentic.

INTEGRITY

Leaders of transformation have a high degree of integrity that increases their credibility as role models (Figure 13-2). The subject of integrity has received considerable attention lately due to several noteworthy incidents of senior executives who, based on their behavior, appear to have a lack of integrity. This lack of integrity has resulted in errors in judgement, resulting in failed business deals and in some cases the loss of the entire firm.

Integrity is freedom. First, there is no need to remember

Figure 13-2 Integrity

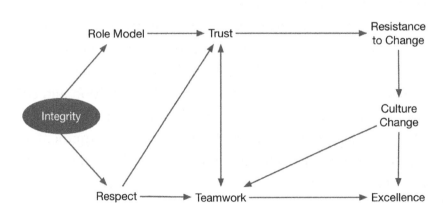

which story was told to which person if you're honest. Second, integrity is associated with a clear conscience and peace of mind. Integrity is the essential ingredient to trust and ultimately teamwork. Why? A person with integrity is genuine, honest, and authentic. You can count on them to tell the truth regardless of the consequences. When a person with integrity treats all people with respect, regardless of station, it is sincere.

SYSTEMS PERSPECTIVE

Organization architects have an uncommon worldview. They view the world as a dynamic system of interrelated components. This view is developed by practicing systems thinking, reflection, and personal learning. In business as in basketball, the outcome doesn't change by watching the scoreboard. The outcome (wins vs. losses) changes when a talented team who get "The Secret" work together to put more balls through the hoop than the opponent. The secret of business is that it isn't about business — it is about making the system of stakeholders successful.

Taking this systems concept beyond teamwork to an organizational level, high-performing companies find the leverage points in their system to create value for multiple stakeholders. In other words, they create an environment for employees (workforce) to achieve their potential and create great experiences for customers (products, services, interactions, etc.) who in turn come back for more (repeat business) and tell their friends (referral business) thus growing the total revenue and profitability which benefits the investors. A system perspective includes an understanding of the cause-and-effect relationships within the organization. For example, an organization might determine that an investment in customer service training will result in improved customer service that, in turn, will result in increased customer satisfaction and then repeat business and referrals.

In the Epilogue of *The Book of Basketball: The NBA According to the Sports Guy*, Bill Walton proposes that The Secret is "A choice." Will you choose to be successful by making your team and stakeholders successful? Are your systems designed to take advantage of key leverage points and create the greatest value for the many stakeholders?

ATTITUDES AND MOTIVATIONS

Why do so many leaders fail to change themselves and do what we know is required to transform their organization systems, culture, and people? One reason is their motivational and attitudinal patterns are often not consistent with the behaviors and activities required by the tasks of organization design and transformation. Organization architects have attitudes and motives that are different from other leaders. According to survey results, successful leaders of transformation are significantly different from other effective leaders on six factors (Larson, Latham, Harshman, and Appleby, 2012).

Successful organization architects:

1. Are less likely to think that having sole responsibility is important. A low need for sole responsibility leads to increased collaboration and teamwork.

2. Are more likely to want to evolve or change and drive continuous improvement. While the transformation CEO may be proud of what the team has accomplished, at the same time, they are never satisfied with the status quo —

no matter how good that may be. In other words, they are never satisfied.

3. Learn from past successes and failure and use those lessons to help develop sustainable organization strategies for the future. Leaders of successful transformation are able to learn from the past, focus on the present execution, and plan for the future. Easier said than done!

4. Are likely to be intolerant of the actions of others when they differ from the organization's vision and values. While failure is tolerated and in some cases celebrated, behavior that is not consistent with the values and vision of the organization are not tolerated.

5. Are strongly motivated to work with systems and processes. Successful leaders of organization design understand the causal chain of engaged employees, quality products and services, customer satisfaction, and financial success.

6. Are strongly motivated to work with facts and knowledge (information). Transformational leaders use detailed information to understand the internal and external systems and environments and develop proactive strategies to succeed in today's complex and dynamic global environment.

Organization architects combine empirical evidence (science) with systems thinking and design thinking to create the organizations they really want. Even if you do not currently possess these attitudes and motivations, there is good news: it is it possible to change your motivations and attitudes.

REFLECTION QUESTIONS

1. Assess your individual characteristics.

Do you find meaning and purpose helping others succeed?

Are you humble, but at the same time confident, in your ability to help others?

Do you have to sacrifice your values to succeed in your organization?

Do you have a systems perspective of the organization and the environment it operates in?

2. Reflect on your attitudes and motivations.

Are you motivated to be in charge and take sole responsibility for the group?

Are you ever satisfied with the organization?

Do you learn from success and failure?

How tolerant are you of people who are not onboard with the mission, vision, and values?

Do you like to work on the organization systems and processes to redesign and improve them?

Do you like working with data and information to improve the organization?

Creating sustainable value for multiple stakeholders is a noble way to run an organization. Those who succeed at transforming their organizations to achieve sustainable excellence are special — special in the sense that they are uncommon but exactly what we need to address the organizational and societal challenges of the 21st century. The good news is you can choose to be a leader of [re]design and transformation and achieve sustainable excellence. It is a choice. That is all it takes to start.

"A journey of 1,000 miles begins with a single step"
— (Tao Te Ching)

14

FACILITATORS OF CHANGE

INTRODUCTION

The journey to [re]design and [re]create an organization is challenging and uncertain. Many change efforts fail to achieve their objectives because leadership fails to set the example and personally see it through to the outcome. But you aren't alone. The collaborative leader develops a team of organization architects and engages them in a collective effort to [re]design the organization. To get this team moving, you will need to leverage the tension (dissatisfaction x compelling vision) and continuously raise the bar as the journey unfolds to maintain that tension. Your task is to create the environment that helps the people in your organization create ever-improving value for multiple stakeholders, including themselves.

While there are many ways to [re]create the organization you really want, there is a logical "form follows function" sequence or path that includes the least amount of rework. The first phase is to build a solid foundation with a leadership team that understands the 14 components of the Leadership and Design Blueprint. That leadership team then develops the enterprise systems model that is the framework for the organization. Once the framework is developed, the next step is to [re]design the top-level systems including customers, production, supplier and partner, workforce, knowledge, leaders and strategy, and governance systems. Only then are you ready to deploy [re] design throughout the organization. We begin with you and your team of organization architects.

TEAM OF ORGANIZATION ARCHITECTS

It takes a team of organization architects to [re]imagine, [re]design, and [re]invent an organization to achieve sustainable excellence. Organization Architects (OAs) come in a wide variety of roles, responsibilities, and backgrounds. There are two main types of OAs — leaders and those who help them. Formal leaders include those leading existing organizations that need to be redesigned and entrepreneurs who are designing the organization for this first time. Those who help them include internal subject matter experts (SMEs) and external consultants.

Becoming a competent OA requires the development of two key skill sets: leadership and design. Even those who help the formal leaders must also be leaders to be effective. Organization Architects are collaborative and leverage the help of both internal SMEs and external consultants to save time and money. While the leadership framework can be designed and implemented without any help from the outside, internal and external consultants or SMEs help facilitate and accelerate organizational transformation. Successful transformations benefit from the support of an internal SME OAs who act as the senior leader's right-hand person during the transformation. Also, external OA consultants help accelerate the learning and improvement process. As the old saying goes, "Time is money!" To get moving, you have to create and maintain enough tension to overcome the inertia of the status quo.

CREATE AND MAINTAIN TENSION

We began this exploration in Chapter 1 with the forces for change to create enough tension to overcome inertia and get going.

Once you get going, and you're working [re]design projects, you start improving. As you improve, the dissatisfaction level goes down and the tension decreases (Figure 14-1). When the tension decreases, you will no longer have enough force to overcome inertia and entropy takes over and you decline again.

Figure 14-1 Maintaining Tension

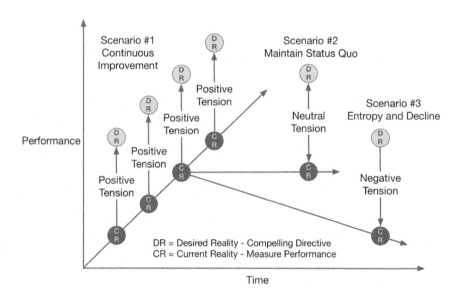

Note: The amount of tension required to maintain the gains depends on the length of time the new practices and cultural norms have been in place.

Maintaining the tension is critical to keeping the organization moving because as soon as people are satisfied, all progress stops. Unfortunately, the world continues to change and if we're happy with where we are, we're going to fall behind and performance will start to decline. Even award-winning organizations have to guard against becoming complacent.

As one CEO noted, "I would always tell our leadership, you know it isn't about winning an award because I had asked them who won the Super Bowl last year, who won the Super Bowl the year before—you know you can't remember." So as the organization improves, the bar has to be continuously raised to maintain the tension. We begin with the leadership team setting the example by developing a solid foundation for the transformation.

DEVELOP A SOLID FOUNDATION

The first step in the journey is for the leadership team to begin their own journey. The leadership team must become the architects of the organization that they really want. Only then will they be credible leaders of the transformation to sustainable excellence. In short, actions speak louder than words. The first step is to understand the 14 components of the Leadership and Design Blueprint. This will begin the journey from fire-fighting to fire prevention. Working through the 14 components in the Leadership and Design Blueprint will provide the structure for developing a common approach to leading. The 14 components also provide a solid foundation for the development and alignment of the organization design cornerstones and culture. When I ask successful organization architects — including CEOs — what they would do differently next time, the most common response is they would have aligned the organization sooner because that was where the real power was.

Four key elements that must be aligned and integrated for any major change effort to succeed are stakeholders, strategy, systems, and scorecard. In fact, the alignment and integration of these four cornerstones with the organizational culture may be the most important facilitator of effective organization [re] design and transformation.

While the four leadership system components of stakeholders, strategy, systems, and scorecard are all interrelated, there is a logical sequence to help you think about the alignment of these components (Figure 14-2). First, identify the stakeholders and their needs, wants, and desires inform the development of strategies for both products and the organization. Then develop strategies to produce both external products and services as well as organization systems to effectively produce and deliver those products and services. Finally, develop a comprehensive scorecard that measures how well the systems and products are working along with the value created for the multiple stakeholders. This is then fed back in a learning loop to the strategy.

Figure 14-2 Alignment of Four Cornerstones

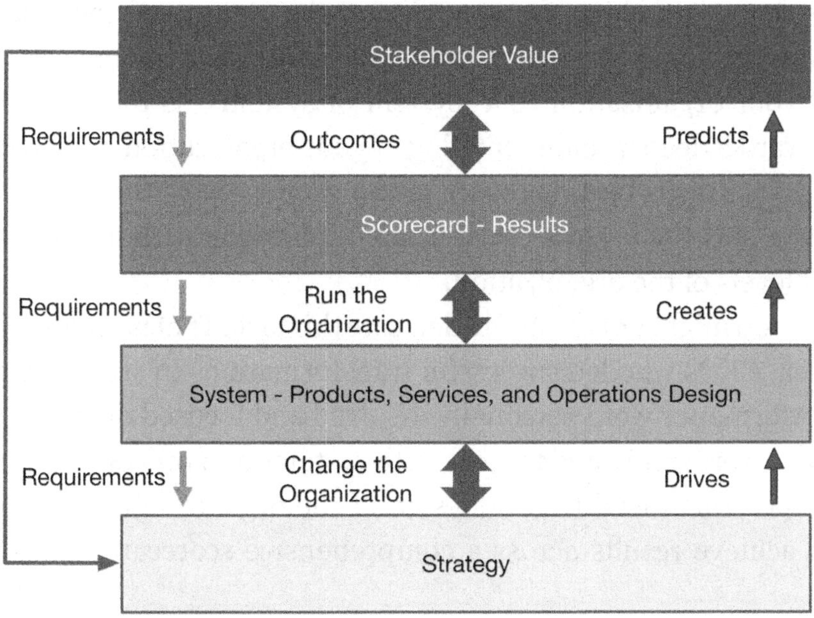

The next step in developing the foundation is to make the desired culture explicit. Identify the key culture components (values, rituals, heroes, and symbols) that will provide the glue between the cornerstones. The alignment of the cultural components is essential to avoid confusion and increase credibility. Finally, develop leaders as organization architects. Identify the leadership activities and behaviors that define leadership for your organization. Then develop leaders at all levels to do these activities in a way that best fits your organization's context, mission, and vision. With a solid foundation in place, you are ready to construct the enterprise systems framework.

CONSTRUCT THE ENTERPRISE FRAMEWORK

With your foundation in place, you are ready to develop an Enterprise Systems Model of your organization. This model is the overarching framework for the design of the major organizational systems. Developing an explicit understanding of your organization as a "system of systems" is the first step toward a deeper understanding of your organization and how it works. This is best done as a group exercise with the executive team and then refined over several iterations with input from all levels of the organization.

You might be tempted to delegate this task. That is a really bad idea. CEOs who led successful transformations to achieve high performance were personally involved and focused on systems. They were motivated to work with systems and processes which helped them lead the [re]design of the organization's systems to achieve results across a comprehensive scorecard (Larson, et al., 2012). This enterprise systems model is the basis for the design or redesign of the individual top-level systems.

[RE]DESIGN TOP-LEVEL SYSTEMS

The third phase in the journey is the [re]design and development of the top-level systems. The enterprise systems model identifies the major systems of the organization but that is the easy part. Now the task is to design those top-level systems. But where should you start? There are two answers to this question. First, you can do a table-top sort of assessment where you identify the strengths and opportunities for improvement for each top-level system. Then, compare the assessments and identify the systems that if [re]designed would make the biggest impact on organization performance. In other words, which system is causing the most "fires"? The second answer is to begin as if you were designing or redesigning the organization from scratch. Not that you will do that, but there is a logical sequence for a first-time design.

The best place to start a top-level system [re]design is with the value creation systems. Ideally we take a "form follows function" approach working from the outside in. Begin with the customer systems first and get the external facing systems that serve the customers [re]designed first. Then develop the production systems and the supplier and partner systems that create the products and services for the customers. Then the workforce systems that support and make the production and customer systems come alive. Then develop the measurement and analysis systems to support fact-based management and improvement. Once the value chain and enabling workforce and measurement systems are developed, focus on the leadership, strategy, and governance systems that guide the work of the organization. At this point in the journey, it is time to spread the [re]design of systems throughout the rest of the organization.

DETAILS AND DEPLOYMENT

The fourth phase is to [re]design and develop the systems, sub-systems, and support systems throughout the organization. The [re]design projects are an opportunity to develop leaders as organization architects throughout your organization. During this phase of the journey each part of the organization identifies their own value creation processes including the customers (internal or external) and suppliers and partners (internal and external).

For many parts of the organization the customer is the next operation. If each part of the organization identifies their customers and their requirements, and validates these with their customers or next operation, the result will be an explicit system or network of internal processes. Leaders who understand the bigger organization system then help identify the connections to develop a complete integrated "picture" of the organization systems.

The journey to becoming the architect of the organization you really want is one of learning and innovation — learning and innovation to design and develop the organization systems throughout the organization. As organization members [re]design their own piece of the organization, they make it better for the stakeholders and more personal for themselves.

Work is personal and one reason so many change efforts fail during the implementation phase is the new design is imposed on the people. Deploying [re]design to all levels in the organization is the equivalent of using their input to design a building and then letting them arrange and decorate their own office or workspace.

CONCLUSION

On the surface, a building is a collection of walls with a foundation, a frame, sheetrock, wires, plumbing, air conditioning, etc. But we don't live and work in the walls. We experience the SPACE that those walls create and surround. A building is a container for space. It creates an environment for humans to interact and communicate. Some have proposed that organizations don't really exist because the organization itself is not very tangible. However, the organization has many tangible artifacts that influence the stakeholders, including documents, policies, strategies, plans, rules, rituals, symbols, and, yes, the physical environment. The people inside the organization experience the combination of these artifacts, which influences their feelings, thoughts, and behavior. In other words, they experience the space or environment that those artifacts create.

The organization then can be thought of as a human-created environment for a group of people to interact and communicate to accomplish a mission. The central design CHALLENGE for the organization architect is to create a humanistic environment that allows multiple stakeholders to create value for others and themselves.

Should you accept the challenge of [re]designing an organization that creates value for multiple stakeholders, make sure you enjoy the journey. There is an old saying, "When you think your journey to excellence is over, it is." The journey to sustainable excellence never ends. The only constant is the need to continuously learn and improve. I hope this book helps you on your journey to [re]create the organization that you really want and society needs.

Enjoy the journey!

John Latham, Ph.D.

REFERENCES

Anderson, R. C. (1998). *Mid-Course Correction - Toward a Sustainable Enterprise: The Interface Model.* White River Junction, VT, Chelsea Green.

AMA. (1991). *Blueprints for Service Quality: The Federal Express Approach.* New York: American Management Association.

Beckhard, R. and R. T. Harris (1987). *Organizational Transitions: Managing Complex Change.* Reading, Massachusetts, Addison-Wesley.

Belasco, J. A. (1990). *Teaching the Elephant to Dance.* New York, NY: Crown Publishers.

Brown, T. (2008). Design Thinking. *Harvard Business Review, 86*(6), 9

Cameron, K. S., & Quinn, R. E. (1999). *Diagnosing and Changing Organizational Culture: Based on the Competing Values Framework.* Reading, MA: Addison-Wesley.

Covey, S. R. (1989). *The 7 Habits of Highly Effective People.* New York, NY: Simon & Shuster.

Deming, W. E. (1986). *Out of the Crisis.* Cambridge: Massachusetts Institute of Technology, Center for Advanced Engineering Study.

Deming, W. E. (1994). *The New Economics: For Industry,*

Government, Education (2nd ed.). Cambridge, MA: Massachusetts Institute of Technology Center for Advanced Engineering Study (MIT CAES).

Drucker, P. F. (2006). *Classic Drucker: Essential Wisdom of Peter Drucker from the Pages of Harvard Business Review.* Boston: Harvard Business Review Press.

Elkington, J., Emerson, J., & Beloe, S. (2006). The Value Palette: A Tool for Full Spectrum Strategy. *California Management Review, 48*(2), 6-28.

Ford, M. W. and J. Evans (2006). "The Role of Follow-up in Achieving Results from Self-Assessment Processes." *The International Journal of Quality & Reliability Management 23*(6), 18.

Freeman, R. E., Harrison, J. S., Wicks, A. C., Parmar, B., & de Colle, S. (2010). *Stakeholder Theory: The State of the Art.* Cambridge: Cambridge University Press.

Fry, L. W., Latham, J. R., Clinebell, S. K. & Krahnke, K. (2016). Spiritual Leadership as a Model for Performance Excellence: A Study of Baldrige Award Recipients. *Journal of Management, Spirituality, and Religion.*

Goldsmith, M., & Morgan, H. (2005). Leadership as a Contact Sport. *Leadership Excellence, 22*(8), 2.

Harter, J. K., Schmidt, F. L., & Hayes, T. L. (2002). Business-Unit-Level Relationship between Employee Satisfaction, Employee Engagement, and Business Outcomes: A Meta-Analysis. *Journal of Applied Psychology, 87*(2), 12.

Hatch, N. W., & Dyer, J. H. (2004). Human Capital and Learning as a Source of Sustainable Competitive Advantage. *Strategic Management Journal, 25*(12), 24.

Heskett, J. L., Jones, T. O., Loveman, G. W., Sasser Jr., W. E., & Schlesinger, L. A. (1994). Putting the Service-Profit Chain to Work. *Harvard Business Review, 72*(2), 164-170.

Hodgetts, R. M., Kuratko, D. F., & Hornsby, J. S. (1999). Quality Implementation in Small Business: Perspectives From the Baldrige Award Winners. *S.A.M. Advanced Management Journal, 64*(1), 11.

Hofstede, G., Hofstede, G. J., & Minkov, M. (2010). *Cultures and Organizations: Software of the Mind.* New York: McGraw Hill.

Kaplan, R. S., & Norton, D. P. (1996). Using the Balanced Scorecard as a Strategic Management System. *Harvard Business Review, 74*(1), 11.

Kotter, J. P., & Heskett, J. L. (1992). *Corporate Culture and Performance.* New York: The Free Press.

Kotter, J. P. (1995). "Leading Change: Why Transformation Efforts Fail." *Harvard Business Review, 73*(2), 9.

Kroll, M. J., Toombs, L. A., & Wright, P. (2000). Napoleon's Tragic March Home from Moscow: Lessons in Hubris. *Academy of Management Executive, 14*(1), 12

Latham, J. R. (2013a). A Framework for Leading the Transformation to Performance Excellence Part I: CEO Perspectives on Forces, Facilitators, and Strategic Leadership Systems. *Quality Management Journal, 20*(2), 22

Latham, J. R. (2013b). A Framework for Leading the Transformation to Performance Excellence Part II: CEO Perspectives on Leadership Behaviors, Individual Leader Characteristics, and Organizational Culture. *Quality Management Journal, 20*(3), 22

Latham, J. R. (2013c). How Much Does Your Organization Weigh? *INNOVATION, 32*(2), 4

Latham, J. R. (2012). Management System Design for Sustainable Excellence: Framework, Practices and Considerations. *Quality Management Journal, 19*(2), 15

Latham, J. R. (1995). Visioning: The Concept, Trilogy, and Process. *Quality Progress, 28*(4), 4

Larson, M., Latham, J. R., Appleby, C. A., & Harshman, C. L. (2012). CEO Attitudes and Motivations: Are They Different for High Performing Organizations? *Quality Management Journal, 19*(4), 15

Lewin, K. (1952) *Field Theory in Social Science: Selected Theoretical Papers*, London: Tavistock.

Lipton, M. (1996) Demystifying the Development of Organizational Vision, *Sloan Management Review 37*(4), 10.

Osterwalder, A. & Y. Pigneur (2010). *Business Model Generation.* Hoboken, NJ, John Wiley & Sons.

Pfeffer, J., & Sutton, R. I. (2006). *Hard Facts, Dangerous Half-Truths and Total Nonsense: Profiting from Evidence-based Management.* Boston: Harvard Business School Press.

Prahalad, C. K., & Hamel, G. (1990). The Core Competence of the Corporation. *Harvard Business Review, 68*(3), 13.

Senge, P. M. (1990). *The Fifth Discipline: The Art and Practice of The Learning Organization*. New York: Currency Doubleday.

Shewhart, W. A. (1931). *Economic Control of Quality of Manufactured Product*. New York: D. Van Nostrand Company.

Simmons, B. (2009). *The Book of Basketball: The NBA According to the Sports Guy*. New York: ESPN Books.

Spong, D. & Collard, D. (2009). *The Making of a World Class Organization*. Milwaukee, Wisconsin: ASQ Press.

UN. (1987). *Report of the world commission on environment and development: Brundtland report*.

Wu, K. -C. (1928). *Ancient Chinese Political Theories*. Shanghai, China: The Commercial Press, Limited

Zimmerer, T. E. & Latham, J. R. (2014). *One size fits all: Servant leadership an effective approach for all generations*. 74th Annual Meeting of the Academy of Management, Philadelphia, Academy of Management.

ABOUT THE AUTHOR

Dr. John Latham is an organization architect with over 35 years of experience working in and with commercial, non-profit, and government organizations around the world. He has enjoyed a diverse professional life from his first adult job with the U.S. Air Force to Vice President of Corporate Quality and Business Excellence for a $1.3  billion *in vitro* diagnostics manufacturer with operations in 40 countries to an international consultant on leadership and design for sustainable excellence.

John is the founder of the Organization Design Studio™ a digital media, education, and design firm focused on helping leaders, entrepreneurs, and the consultants who help them, create the organizations they really want. His firm focuses on innovative ways to design organizations and systems that create value for multiple stakeholders including investors, customers, employees, suppliers and partners, society, and the natural environment.

John has designed a wide variety of organization systems and processes from leadership and strategic management systems to production systems to measurement and analysis systems. He has worked with a variety of organizations including several Baldrige Award recipients across several industries: commercial, non-profit, healthcare, education, and start-ups. Some of his clients have included Boeing, Kawasaki, Tata Consultancy Services (TCS), The Ritz-Carlton, British Airways, Motorola, U. S. Department of Energy, Lockheed Martin, U. S. Defense Depot San Joaquin, U.S. Technology Resources, Poudre Valley Health System, Long Beach Unified School District, VA Cooperative Studies, Pro-Tec Coating Company, Monfort College of Business, and Virtjoule, Inc.

He has published scientific and technical papers on leading transformation and the design of organizations and systems in several journals including *INNOVATION* and *Quality Management Journal.* He is a two-time recipient of the Gryna Award from the American Society for Quality for publishing the paper that made the largest contribution to the extension of understanding and knowledge of philosophy, principles, or methods of quality management during the previous year (2013 and 2014).

John served as a judge/examiner for several, organization excellence award programs. He served as a judge for the Colorado Performance Excellence Award, the Robert W. Carey VA Healthcare Award, and the Army Communities of Excellence Award. He served as an examiner for the Malcolm Baldrige National Quality Award for nine years and led site visits to some of the nation's highest performing companies. He also served as an honored assessor for the JRD TATA QV Award in India.

He lives near the base of the Rocky Mountains in Monument, Colorado with his wife Penny. They have three grown children and one grandson.

FREE STUDIO MEMBERSHIP

Get the Tools You Need to [Re]Create the Organization You Really Want!™

Sign up for your Free Studio Membership and get access to the free eBook **Library**, online access to the **Blueprints** Section, and email updates when new **Articles** are posted. We promise not to spam you or give/sell your email to anyone, ever!

http://organizationdesignstudio.com/free-studio-membership

Made in the USA
Middletown, DE
12 September 2021